STAFF APPRAISAL

A first step to effective leadership

Gerry Randell is Senior Lecturer in Occupational Psychology and Chairman of the Undergraduate School of Managerial Sciences at the University of Bradford Management Centre. He is Editor of the *International Review of Applied Psychology* and Chairman of the Independent Assessment and Research Centre, London.

Peter Packard and **John Slater** are directors of SMT Limited and of Tweed Management Services Ltd, Southend, specializing in management skills training and consultancy. Until 1981 they were both with Fisons Ltd, Group Training Department.

The authors acknowledge the wisdom and experience of Ray Shaw of Fisons plc whose practical contribution to the original work was crucial to the development of this approach

STAFF APPRAISAL

A first step to effective leadership

Gerry Randell · Peter Packard
John Slater

Institute of Personnel Management

Previously published as *Staff Appraisal*
First edition 1972, revised 1974
This edition 1984

Note: wherever appropriate the convention has been
followed whereby *he* and *him* are used to cover *she* and *her*.

Phototypeset by Latimer Trend & Company Ltd,
Plymouth and printed in Great Britain by Dotesios
Printers, Bradford-on-Avon

British Library Cataloguing in Publication Data

Randell, Gerry
  Staff appraisal: a first step to effective leadership. —3rd
  ed.
  1. Employees, Rating of
  I. Title   II. Packard, Peter   III. Slater, John
  658.3'125   HF5549.5.R5

ISBN 0-85292-333-3

Contents

II Improving staff appraisal through training

Preface to the third edition

We have been very encouraged by the way this book has been used by many members of the IPM and organizations throughout the world to help planning and decision making about staff development procedures. When it was first written in 1972 the intention was to guide thinking rather than answer questions, and to balance the practice of staff appraisal with a conceptual analysis of the process. From discussions at IPM conferences, with generations of students and thousands of managers on the two-day workshops described in this book, this objective appears to have been achieved.

Organizational practices and academic concepts do not stand still. Consequently, the major outcome from all this work is the growing awareness of just how important, and complex, is the skill of interacting purposefully with people at work. It is this *skills approach* to staff appraisal and development that has been the major influence on work organizations, on our research and thinking about managerial behaviour and in the structure and content of the teaching material and practical work described in this third edition.

It is interesting to note that, starting from the analysis of what should go on within an organization's staff appraisal system, we have travelled a path which converges with efforts to understand the concept and practice of leadership. Comments about the former has led to the realization that the skill of adding to the capacity and motivation of people to carry out their existing job is a crucial part of leadership activity.

More effective leadership results from applying the skills of data-based decision making described in this book. The increased commitment and motivation to work which results from the application of such skills will benefit leader, subordinate and organization alike. This is why we have added the sub-title to this book.

Many changes have occurred in both the external and internal industrial environments so we have felt it important to review carefully the precise relevance of the principles and concepts of the original editions to the conditions of the mid 1980s.

In the early 1970s the process of staff appraisal took place in a period of relatively static employment. Employees were rarely dismissed and those whose performance was no longer satisfactory were moved to a position where they could do only a limited amount of harm. Having recruited employees, most companies took care to keep them. They provided the best conditions of service they could afford, then encouraged them to grow with the company and developed them, not only to fill future vacancies but to fulfil employees' ambitions all for fear that they might otherwise move on. In those circumstances it was not always easy to convince management that the overall objective of the staff appraisal process was to improve performance. Often it was regarded as a way of keeping employees happy, ie a product of personnel bureaucracy.

The economic recession of the late '70s and early '80s produced far-reaching changes, not least of which was the discovery that large numbers of employees must, and more importantly, *could* be dispensed with. Large lump-sum payments and early retirement pensions mitigated any imagined threats of organized opposition. Redundancy became so common-place that corporate images were not unduly dented.

This had a highly significant effect on the power balance between employers and employees in many industries. Real or imaginary threats were no longer feared, nor was the potential loss of any but key employees. Succession plans and career development systems were rendered invalid overnight by wholesale restructuring. Far from caring about their futures or their careers the majority of employees were thankful merely for the preservation of their jobs.

Later it was clear that a new era had arrived. Its presence was most noticeable by the emergence of a new breed of top management, concerned only with the realities and not the façade. Empires had been dismantled, authority developed, entrepreneurs appointed or promoted. Adventurism, opportunism, resourcefulness and sheer professionalism were the objectives for survival. The fat had been shed and all were determined to stay lean.

These changes have an important bearing on the resulting attitudes of employees and management. Insecurity is likely to be a dominant factor and the evidence of the speed and scale of organizational changes will die hard. Career opportunities are fewer with more people waiting to fill them; élitism will increase and so will obsolescence. Management will, and can, demand tougher personnel policies.

It is inevitable that these conditions, if not properly managed, will produce a demoralized but compliant workforce motivated by fear rather than commitment. Results will be achieved but those results are likely to fall short of their potential and require more management time and effort than would be achieved by a workforce that is both self-motivated and committed. It is to these objectives that the process of staff appraisal and hence better leadership is directed.

We conclude that there is never a more relevant time for the active use of staff appraisal. Also that the level of skill required at the present time by both experienced and new managers has had to rise still further to cope with the constraints which the current climate imposes. It simply is not good enough to assume that managers automatically acquire a 'Jacob's coat' of skills; appraisal skill is the first stripe amongst many to be acquired through training.

Part I
The basic principles

I
Introduction

Basic concepts

The management of people at work is most concerned with managing the interaction between what is inside people, ie human capacities, inclinations and needs, and what is within work, ie the quantity and quality of 'output' and the satisfaction that people can get from their job.

In theory there is no real need for a manager at all. Many people can be heard denying their usefulness even to the extent that workers would be able to perform better without them. However, the history of 'self-managing cooperatives' indicates there is still a need for at least *skilful* managers. The real question is, what should a manager do that aids this interaction between people and their work? Staff appraisal is one of those occasions when an organization sanctions and encourages the expenditure of time and effort by both a manager and a member of staff for a formal 'interaction' aimed at improving the performance of the individual, the organization and the manager, at their respective tasks. The sadness of much staff appraisal activity is that what could be a positively encouraged occasion for improving the interaction between individuals and their employers frequently turns out to be dysfunctional, ie relationships would have been better if the appraisal had not taken place. It was this observation that led to the work behind our original book in 1972, and no doubt, is the spur for many readers of this edition.

So what can be done to improve the appraisal process beyond what would happen if well-selected staff were left to develop themselves? What is the skill of staff development? How can managers be encouraged to develop and apply this skill? It is to these issues that this book is addressed.

Overview

People go to work to apply their capacities, inclinations and needs to the objectives of their employing organization to produce goods and services in economic quantity and quality and, if they are so minded, for the organization also to provide satisfaction for their employees. It is this interaction that is there to be managed. Three main outcomes can be observed from this interaction, as indicated in figure 1 below.

Alienation: if the interaction goes badly wrong, then employees can become 'switched off'. Feelings of exploitation, disregard and under-utilization can produce this outcome, in which both sides 'lose' and suffer.
Conflict: if misunderstandings arise, interests clash, or appreciation is not displayed, then antagonism is produced. At best, only one side 'wins' and gains at the expense of the other.
Motivation: if balance is obtained between what is 'inside' the 'individual' and what is required by the organization then the

Figure 1

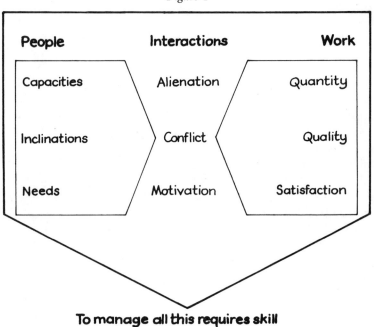

To manage all this requires skill

elusive phenomenon of 'motivation' is experienced. It is important to note that motivation here is regarded as an 'outcome' rather than a cause, ie it arises from a balanced interaction rather than causing the interaction to happen.

This 'overview' of the process of personal management has many practical implications. The first is that what has been described is similar to what the 'leadership' theorists are attempting to explain and, therefore understanding the process is the first step to better leadership.

The diagram illustrates the purpose of the process of staff appraisal, for it can be seen as the formally decreed occasion when information bearing on all the headings in figure 1 is exchanged. This purpose first led to the setting up of the *annual* 'appraisal interview', still prevalent in many organizations. It is now widely acknowledged that this interview should be operational as frequently as thought necessary and desirable by a manager or a member of staff. Judging the frequency for such an interaction is just another aspect of the skill. Consequently the appraisal system should be regarded as the usual 'human resources management' review. It is not the thing that has to be done once a year because 'personnel says we have to'. It is the main, formally sanctioned activity, over and above the daily operational contact that managers have with their staff, to review and discuss *exactly* what goes on, and what *should* go on between an employee and an employing organization. The experience and research (listed in the bibliography) on which this book is based, can be summarized under the following six key headings:

PURPOSEFUL MANAGEMENT

The need and opportunity for comprehensive and precise communication to take place within organizations are often expressed, and many methods to achieve this have been described. However, none of them are as effective as a skilfully conducted 'conversation with a purpose' between people. This interview, if conducted with the clear and explicit purpose of improving the ability of staff in their existing jobs, will maintain and, possibly, increase, their willingness to apply their full abilities to their job.

So, for the manager, the appraisal process encourages the assembly of information that allows for information-based decision making about staff.

5

For the managed, appraisal gives the opportunity for injecting information into the organization.

Learning with precision

Communication in organizations is necessary, but not sufficient to bring about change. The transfer of information should lead to learning, and it is the opportunity for gaining precision in understanding what is being said which is the main advantage of the interview over all other methods of communication. This is why a tutorial is more effective than a lecture, a discussion more productive than a memo.

So, for a manager, appraisal provides the opportunity to learn exactly what the staff feel about themselves in relation to their jobs and to understand the crucial factors affecting their current level of motivation and what can be done to maintain or add to it.

For the managed, it is the opportunity to learn exactly what is required to be done differently so that the manager would think better of the performance. In other words, to acquire that addition to capacity that would have the most immediately beneficial effect on the current level of performance.

Committed action plans

Again, learning in any applied field comes to nothing unless it is translated into an action plan. This is where the techniques of 'targetting' or 'management by objectives' can be useful. How the learning and translation process is conducted is crucial in determining whether or not the action plan has commitment attached to it, or merely compliance. It may take longer, but once obtained, commitment is more satisfying for the managed, for they feel that their needs are being understood and acted upon; and more satisfactory for the managers for they know that their staff will try to meet their objectives or targets without checks or threats.

Segregating assessment

Assessment and performance improvement should be segregated. It is the confusion between these which appears to

6

undermine the success of appraisal. Somehow, perhaps due to training in the sciences and in accountancy, many managers find it hard to understand that the process of assessment is an unnecessary, difficult and dangerous approach to changing behaviour at work.

It is not necessary to 'measure' behaviour at work before attempting to change it. All that is required is to decide what aspect of a person's performance needs to be changed, ie diagnosis; then an exact prescription of the new behaviour defined, ie 'treatment'. Measurements are sometimes required to feed into an organization's merit-rating or potential spotting procedure or to let an employee learn 'exactly where I stand'. Unnecessary and frequently undesirable complications arise in those appraisal systems built around assessment procedures, such as various forms of rating scales. Such procedures force the managers to make and report some kind of quantitative assessment of the work of their staff, or even worse, the extent of possession of an organizationally valued personality trait, as the basis of the staff appraisal scheme. Such procedures are invariably fraught with danger. More pointedly, they divert managers from the essential developmental components of staff appraisal, and they encourage the managed to be suspicious and defensive. The history of staff appraisal schemes shows that the most frequent reason for their failure is the application of conceptually muddled attempts at measuring people.

If and when assessments of performance are required, they should be carried out through technically sound procedures, such as behaviourally anchored rating scales or standardized psychological and attainment tests, and by thoroughly briefed and trained staff.

The clearest outcome of all the research on staff appraisal is the need to separate assessment from performance improvement to make an appraisal scheme really work. Of course, if an organization only requires its appraisal scheme to feed information into mechanistic merit-rating or promotion-determining procedures, then an evaluative appraisal procedure may meet such requirements. If, however, staff appraisal is expected to improve the performance of people in their existing jobs, then the first thing to cut out of existing schemes, or the last thing to build into new schemes, is the attempt to 'measure' performance or 'assess' personality.

7

TRAINING IN SELF-DEVELOPMENT

The more appraisal skills have been studied, the more it has become apparent that they are a very complex and high-level activity. They appear to fall into that class of skills, like reading and writing, that, after initial training and experience, are easy for most people to do but, ultimately, exceedingly difficult to do well. The two-day workshop, described on page 113 has now been experienced by thousands of managers and, as the studies later show, appear to have worked in adding to the participants' level of skill. However, no skill of any consequence can be adequately enhanced by just two days training, no matter how powerful the experience.

The experience gained during the 14 years since the first workshop led to the training becoming more concerned with inculcating within managers the facility for self-analysis and self-feedback. Managers should therefore find that their staff development skills improve as a result of practice with their own staff. At the same time, it must not be forgotten that 'managers' are also 'managed'. One of the important outcomes of the change is the way it encourages self-development in all aspects of work. There is little doubt that the skill of self-development is an even more complex and higher level skill than coaching other people, as many tutors and coaches will readily admit. What has become obvious is that the skills of staff and self-development are a very underdeveloped area of academic research.

ORGANIZATIONAL DEVELOPMENT

Much has been written in recent years about the process of organizational development (OD). The writers imply that this is achieved by 'interventions' that lead to more 'openness', 'participation', 'communication' and 'frankness' within organizations. Such changes can be brought about at the structural and procedural levels, but they can be more readily brought about by direct interaction between management and staff, if the skills are there to do it. Staff appraisal is the process through which such changes can be implemented. The design of systems, forms, reporting procedures and allocating time for the appraisal interview are all direct initiatives that can be taken by senior management to develop the organization. The initiative starts from the top, but it will come to nothing if the 'system' does not encourage the practice of skilful interaction between every individual and his manager. To attempt to solve behavioural problems with structural solutions is an inefficient and costly approach to organizational development.

Some kind of staff appraisal activity goes on in all organizations. It ranges from intermittent, informal and often ill-informed discussion between managers about individual members of staff to highly formal appraisal procedures, based on extensive sets of forms and established times, rules and frequency of assessments.

It is hoped that this book will be most relevant to managers who wish to turn an existing *passive* staff appraisal scheme into an *active* one. Many existing staff appraisal procedures can at best be called passive in that they prevent a deterioration in staff performance, thus containing a managerial problem. In such schemes information about individuals is collected imprecisely; staff know about the procedure and are careful in their behaviour: the effect is therefore to maintain a level of performance. These passive schemes are widespread in British industry and many organizations are now considering what can be done to make them more active. An active scheme is one which *adds* to the level of performance of people in the organization. Its essential feature is the assembly and sharing of information, which provides both the individual and organization with a learning experience. This book attempts to provide a bridge between passive and active staff appraisal and development schemes.

The approach emphasizes the practical objectives of staff appraisal procedures rather than trying to apply any theoretical views about what makes people work as they do. But theoretical issues will not be ignored and, where relevant, accumulated knowledge about the behaviour of people at work will be drawn upon, although not explicitly quoted. The aim is to review the concepts and practices of staff appraisal procedures in a way which will help their development in a particular organization.

Although sound concepts are necessary, staff appraisal is essentially a part of a manager's range of skills: improvement will only come through training in these skills. The development of a new system or procedure based on accepted objectives and using a set of agreed documents is an important precursor to improvement in staff appraisal and development practices. But this is secondary to improving staff appraisal procedures by developing the individual manager's skills. The book advances this view on the basis that, in the managerial chain of direction and control, how well a manager develops his staff is the final, and perhaps most important, link in the managerial effectiveness of any organization.

The book focuses upon the interaction between a manager and his staff. It is hoped that the accumulated ideas and experience will help organizations to strengthen and build upon this vital relationship with the individual.

A mass of myth and assertion surrounds the purpose and technique of staff appraisal. A selected bibliography at the end of the book provides key references in this field. It indicates that little hard research has been done on the subject mainly because of the extreme difficulty involved. Surveys have been made of the effectiveness of staff appraisal procedures and some have been published. What seems to emerge is that one kind of procedure may be appropriate to a particular organization at a particular stage in its development, but there is clearly no general strategy which is appropriate to all organizations at all stages of their development. Anyone who has to develop a staff appraisal procedure must therefore judge what is relevant and useful to his organization at that time, and also what would be acceptable to its members. These are important and difficult constraints to handle and beyond the scope of this book.

The work described is open to the same criticism that can be made of other writing in this field in that it is based on assertion rather than research. But the concepts, ideas and practice described are based on a certain amount of 'action research'. The ideas gathered together have been derived from various studies which have been undertaken, and from attempts made to introduce staff appraisal procedures in different organizations (see the 'Bradford' bibliography at the end of the book). The concepts were crystallized as a result of discussion with members of the Institute of Personnel Management's course on staff appraisal and development. The early practical experience of applying the concepts set out in part I are accumulated and followed up by the group training department of Fisons Ltd. This work is described in part II.

If any particular point is emphasized it is that decisions

made about human behaviour at work should be based on information: data must be substituted for theory, mythology, assertion and idealism. Decisions made about people should be based on information about and from those people. This approach can be labelled 'data-based personnel management'. It means that staff appraisal and development should be based on sufficient, relevant and objective information. Unfortunately this is easier said than done but it is the basic principle behind much of what is said in this book. The other theme is the view that organizations can more readily be developed through people than through procedures. The practical implication is that, no matter how good the procedure, it is useless if the individuals involved are not prepared to carry it out.

The converse is also accepted as true: regardless of the inadequacies of the procedures, able and willing staff can produce high quality and effective work within an organization. It therefore follows that if an organization is to be improved emphasis, if not priority, should be given to attempting to improve the people who make it up. This is perhaps the key principle of human resources management.

It should also be said that any procedure in the field of human resources management should not be static. If the aim is to make an organization more effective through making its individual members more effective, the process must be cumulative and continuous. As soon as one level of improvement is reached another emerges, and the strategies for that particular level may not be the same as for the earlier one. Consequently any procedure that is established must be open to change and as soon as it has served its purpose it must be altered. All static procedures can be an enormous constraint on individual and organizational development. An effective human resources management procedure is thus one which has had a facility built into it which can bring its change and development.

Finally, a policy issue should be raised. It depends on whether organizations are established primarily to meet corporate objectives or those of the individuals making them up: not only the individuals at the head of an organization but at all levels. Clearly some kind of balance must be achieved between these two conflicting groups of objectives. It would be comforting to suppose that organizational and individual needs ran parallel rather than antagonistically to each other. Where this is so the appropriate policy decisions are easy to make. But there are many areas where the needs of the individual conflict with those of the organization and a decision has to be made between the two. There are also ethical problems. Just how much should a manager know about his staff? How should this information be stored? Who should have access to it? And there is the whole question of 'manipulation'. These are real issues and care needs to be taken to ensure that *ethical* limits are not exceeded, quite apart from those defined by the Data Protection Act 1984. It is outside the scope of this book to attempt more than to mention that they exist and are important.

Any staff appraisal and development procedure may well be a compromise if the personnel policy decrees that individual and organizational needs should be balanced. Judgement must therefore be exercised by the person who has to develop an existing staff appraisal procedure. If this book helps such people to make a better judgement it will have achieved its purpose.

Purposes

Staff appraisal procedures have many different purposes. Unfortunately, there is a confusion of terms and meanings. The phrase means many things to many people and often has an emotive ring, if the evaluation side is emphasized. In broad terms staff appraisal can be defined as any procedure which helps the collecting, checking, sharing, giving and using of information collected from and about people at work for the purposes of adding to their performance at work.

All appraisal procedures aim at developing people and/or organizations by using information about the behaviour of people at work. All assume that an organization will be more effective as a result of a staff appraisal procedure. The purposes vary from 'organization-centred' to 'individual-centred' and are mainly concerned with establishing controls on the behaviour of people or bringing about change in their behaviour by:

(a) *evaluation:* to enable the organization to share out the money, promotions and perquisites apparently 'fairly'
(b) *auditing:* to discover the work potential, both present and future, of individuals and departments

(c) *constructing succession plans:* for manpower, departmental and corporate planning

(d) *discovering training needs:* by exposing inadequacies and deficiencies that could be remedied by training

(e) *motivating staff:* to reach organizational standards and objectives

(f) *developing individuals:* by advice, information and attempts at shaping their behaviour by praise or punishment

(g) *checking:* the effectiveness of personnel procedures and practices.

Study of existing staff appraisal procedures often shows that these purposes have not been made explicit. They may overlap and merge and sometimes even conflict with each other. They can be analysed and categorized to fall into three main groups of purposes of direct relevance to the manager's task.

The first group relates to the problem of the allocation and distribution of the fruits of organizational activity, such as pay, power, status, self-fulfilment, freedom and all the other kinds of rewards and benefits that membership of an organization can mean to a particular individual. This group of purposes can be achieved through *reward reviews*.

The second group of activities relates to the need to improve the performance of each individual member of staff. The assumption can be made that if at any moment, each individual making up an organization is getting better at his job, the organization is developing and becoming more effective; therefore information is required and a procedure is necessary to bring this about. This kind of managerial activity can be grouped under the general heading of *performance reviews*.

Predicting the level and type of work that the individual will be capable of doing in the future, and how long he will take to achieve this, makes up the third group of staff appraisal purposes. Information can be assembled about a person's past attainments, his current performance and his personal aspirations. A judgement can then be made and plans for his future drawn up which not only fit in with his own ambitions but also with the staffing needs of the organization. This procedure can be described as a *potential review*.

These three groups of activities overlap and interlock to a certain extent but can and should be separated in practice, because the techniques, procedures and information required satisfactorily to achieve each are not necessarily the same. If they are forced to be identical, inaccurate and unfortunate decisions may result from using information which is inadequate to the particular purpose being served.

Many of the managerial problems which exist today can be traced to the association in the minds of people at work, between their work performance, rewards and subsequent promotion. There would be fewer difficulties and less discontent if people at work thought that they should be rewarded and placed in different kinds of jobs according to their capacities and inclinations rather than their current level of performance.

The three groups of activities should also be kept separate in practice because each is exceedingly difficult to do well. To ask a line manager at one sitting to appraise a person's performance, evaluate it and then predict what he would be capable of in the future is more than a highly trained specialist could be expected to do. The burden on the manager and the risk to the individual should therefore not be imposed. All three groups certainly need to be achieved and co-ordinated. But if a successful procedure is to have a chance of developing, an organization should break its existing procedures into three.

The tripartite split can perhaps also be made in responsibilities for each procedure. Responsibility for ensuring that the performance of each individual worker is improved rests squarely with the managers. That for ensuring that the rewards of the organization are shared fairly and agreeably rests with whoever designs and runs the pay and salary administration schemes (such as the staff or industrial relations manager). Responsibility for spotting and using potential must rest with a central human resources or management development department (group personnel or establishment officer). Organizations attempting to develop their staff appraisal and development procedures are strongly advised to plan to keep the three activities of *performance, reward* and *potential review* not only separate in time but also in paper work, procedure and responsibility.

Another group of organizational needs can be identified and is rather specialized; the assembly of information used to evaluate, validate or check the effectiveness of any personnel procedures and practices that the organization has set up. A pertinent example is the evaluation of the effectiveness of a staff appraisal scheme. The kind of information required can be drawn from the other three but usually more information must be collected and analysed if personnel procedures are to be effectively evaluated. Those activities and procedures which bear upon this need can be called *organization reviews*. This is specialized work more akin to that of personnel researchers than human resources managers but is a useful and stimulating discipline for managers to undertake.

Examples of attempts at *organization review* are given in part II. Chapter 6 describes data-gathering about existing appraisal procedures by means of an interview survey of managers. Chapter 10 gives an account of questionnaire surveys of the training established to meet the shortcomings of the existing procedure. Such *organization reviews* need not be elaborate or very statistical to be useful. They can be set up to provide feedback information which will enable any management procedure to be monitored. But once it is intended to go beyond direct monitoring, such reviews can call for sophisticated data collection and analysis techniques. This book must limit itself to encouraging the use of *organization reviews*, leaving the details to other texts.

Perhaps the main reason for keeping these different review procedures separate is a negative one. As stressed, it is difficult to do each of them well. They all involve the most complex resource of all, man and woman. Unlike the other resources available to an organization this is the only one that, if left alone, will grow in its capacity to serve. Machines will rust or wear out, money will become less valuable, markets will be invaded, but people will learn, become wiser and even more 'stable'.

Because people are an adaptable resource, they will put up with a considerable amount of mishandling, particularly if it is benevolent. But the resource may become intractable, alienated and perhaps impossible to manage if crude and uncaring methods of control are used.

Unless formal human resources management procedures can be skilfully applied, it is probably better not to introduce any. Staff appraisal procedures demand skill to work well; they should be kept simple and within the range and ability of practising managers. Rather than attempting to achieve everything at once, the purposes should be grouped into separate procedures and planned, trained for and carried out as individual exercises. There can be central control and co-ordination but line managers should be helped through a well-designed set of procedures to manage their human resources within their own skill capacity. They cannot be expected to give rewards, improve performance, increase motivation and spot and release potential through a single procedure. There is a strong tendency in many organizations to build an all-embracing, monolithic appraisal system. If this book achieves anything, it should at least indicate the failings of such theoretically attractive but practically undesirable staff development schemes.

The basic principles behind the three main groups of appraisal activities will be dealt with in separate sections. As *organization reviews* are so specialized they will not be discussed further. *Performance reviews* are seen as the most important to staff management in organizations. *Reward reviews* and *potential reviews* are more relevant to the problem of 'organization management'. As this book is directed at working through people rather than organizations, *reward reviews* and *potential reviews* will be discussed as essential precursors to effective performance reviews. They are seen as activities that need high-level, detailed policy decisions. An agreed framework and procedure can be established so that managers can work within a clear set of rules and practices about rewards and long-term promotion prospects. They are then able to give their main effort to the major managerial task, that of maintaining and improving the performance of each individual.

2
Reward reviews

Granting pay increases or giving promotions is the whole purpose of any staff appraisal scheme to many organizations. The review consists of an annual interview when a manager announces the 'reward' that a member of staff is to get for his last year's work and the organization's expectations for his future. It should be clear by now that this is regarded as just a part, albeit an important part, of a whole set of reasons for establishing a staff appraisal and development procedure.

Sharing out organizational rewards is a source of considerable conflict and difficulty. The aim is always to minimize the problems in this task and various payment schemes and job evaluation techniques have been developed to help managers. Unfortunately there is as yet no scheme which is universally applicable or acceptable. The problem remains and organizations must do the best they can with the inadequate systems available. The difficulty is to establish a scheme which is at least acceptable to individual members of staff and which will provide scope for meeting employees' expectations.

Again, the problem is one of judgement based on as much objective information as is available and on the awareness of staff expectations. Any reward review scheme should be planned so that such information can be collected and to increase the chances that fair and acceptable reward decisions are made.

The onus for establishing an effective reward review procedure rests squarely on the organization. The whole problem of salary, promotion and privileges policy should be thrashed out and settled; procedures and techniques established to operate the policy; and responsibility allocated to an individual, eg a salary administration, staff relations, industrial relations, personnel, or 'come-what-may' manager so that the system may be continuously updated and monitored. The burden of negotiating any major change in reward level with an individual member of staff should be removed from his immediate manager's area of responsibility. The major role of a manager in the reward review procedure is that of communicating between individuals and the organization that employs them.

The reward policy of the organization may leave a small proportion of the overall reward granted at the manager's disposal as in a 'merit-rating' procedure. Although relatively small, such gifts may have significant symbolic value since they may signal publicly how 'successful' an individual is in the eyes of the organization. But such additional reward procedures may alienate rather than motivate. Another area of leadership is devising, agreeing, maintaining and administering appropriate reward procedures throughout the organization.

This is just one example of an area where the need to share out the fruits of organizational activity can come into conflict with the need to motivate employees. The problem of motivation will be considered in the performance review section. Motivation will be even more difficult to handle if aggravated by an inadequate reward review procedure. Unfortunately the problem will not be solved by a perfect reward review procedure, even if such were possible.

Objectives

The objectives of this particular area of management are to assemble information and to establish a procedure, so that the organization can share out the rewards it has to give, in an acceptable way and, if possible, in a fair and technically sound way too. The organization's immediate objective is to attempt to remove any conflict or alienation which may exist amongst the staff about the sharing out of rewards, and then to create a more general feeling of well-being and satisfaction with the organization.

The word 'morale' is often applied to the feeling which exudes from an apparently satisfied staff of an organization. Morale is one of those concepts like 'beauty' or 'freedom', which can be observed when it is present and noticed when it is absent but precise definition is difficult. This is why reward review procedures are so difficult to establish; it is not possible to be precise about the desired outcomes of a successful procedure. Firms of consultants and various procedures exist to help organizations to establish reward review systems which apparently work. Morale is also of interest to industrial relations specialists where there are strong sociological implications, and to salary administration consultants where there are severe technical difficulties in attempting to measure the worth of jobs and/or individuals. The field of job evaluation, payment by results and merit-rating exists to help managers with the problems of sharing out pay, status, perks and other organizational rewards.

From a staff appraisal point of view, it is important that the manager should know how particular members of staff feel about the reward they are actually getting, and how far their economic and psychological needs are being met by the organization. Where possible the manager should relate this information to the objective data available. Sometimes nothing can be done. The system is so constraining that it is impossible to make any changes. Nevertheless the whole effort of attempting to find out what individuals think about their rewards can sometimes help considerably in ameliorating any conflict or alienation which exists. Members of staff are usually remarkably resilient, adaptive and accommodating. The fact that they know other people are aware of their expectations and needs can sometimes do a great deal to make them feel better if these are not being met.

The main objective of a reward review procedure is thus to clear the ground and lay the foundations for effective performance review procedures. At the same time the procedure should generate information which will enable the organization to share out its rewards more fairly, if not at the time then in the future.

Sources of information

The range of possible reward review decisions open to a manager is set by the policies of the organization. Sometimes the range is extremely wide and is virtually open to hard bargaining and negotiation between individual members of staff and their managers. But more frequently a set of formulae and decision rules determine an individual's rewards. It is rare for such rules to cover completely all the rewards that an organization has to give to an individual member of staff. Something is always left to the discretion of the manager. Here the manager needs to collect the information on all which he is to base his decision about the rewards for a particular individual.

It can be assumed that all the information needed to make any mechanistic decision needed for a job evaluation, incentive or merit-rating system is generated and used by that system. The manager simply 'rubber-stamps' the decision.

For the remainder, the manager must at least know the basic statistics about the distribution of the particular reward amongst comparable groups of staff to be managed. If the reward is a special bonus, increment or perk, the manager must know how many other people received it and what basic parameters, such as age, length of service or special responsibilities applied. A company grapevine can be extremely effective in generating half-truths about such statistics. The manager must have the real figures. The wages department or personnel office should be the source.

The next set of information required is comparative data on how well the individual has performed during the review period *vis à vis* other comparable members of staff. This is extremely delicate and difficult data to assemble. Some organizations develop graphic or multiple step scales and accumulate reports on each member of staff. Some have tried 'self' and 'peer' ratings, ie reports from and about each member of staff asking them to make judgements and comparisons. The decision needs to be made whether managers are to go beyond their own direct observations as a source of comparative information about staff performance.

Whatever the sources, some kind of documentation will be required on which to assemble and collect this information.

Reward review documents

A record card showing salary progression, promotion and perquisites allocation that the individual has experienced during his appointment in the organization is the basic document needed for a systematic reward review procedure. The other side of the card can record job evaluation information about the particular positions held, merit rating awards and any inter-firm comparison data relevant to the particular job. This becomes the basic record document for the individual's rewards from the organization. Space for brief notes about the reward review interviews held between the manager and a particular member of staff can be attached to the card, or part of it if it is a large one. This can be an 'open' document because there can be few serious objections to an individual seeing and reading the contents of the card. It remains within the department, possibly in the confidential files of the departmental head. The basic data about salary and promotion progression is also held in a central record by the wages department and/or personnel office, bearing in mind the technical and ethical problems of record systems mentioned earlier.

A case could be made for some kind of observation sheet as well, to be used for recording assessments of the individual through the review period. This could contain various rating scales, summarizing the observations on a set of scales which the organization values. The text books abound with examples of this type of checklist report form. This kind of apparently objective assessment procedure is popular with designers of mechanistic appraisal procedures. Unfortunately many managers hide behind the apparent objectivity of the scales, and many members of staff object to being assessed on global scales. The thought of being graded or allocated to a certain category of performance can be upsetting to some people. Such procedures can be justified on the ground that they give pleasure to the successful and act as a spur to the less successful. This may be so for some but organizations should ask themselves whether there are not more effective, and perhaps more humane, ways of giving praise and improving the poor performer.

In the absence of skilful management reward giving should be so controlled that it becomes virtually mechanistic and thus automatic. Increasing motivation and improving performance are *not* functions of reward reviews. If they result from such procedures, this is a bonus, and is a sign that a reward review is more than achieving its objectives.

Reward review interview

The reward review is often regarded in some organizations as *the* annual appraisal interview. It is the meeting with the manager when the individual's performance is discussed, mainly to justify any additional reward, or lack of it, which the organization or the manager has decided to give. There is an obvious need for this to take place and to be done well. But it is poor management practice to think that this is the only occasion when an individual's performance need be discussed.

If the reward review interview is handled badly this can present a major problem. The interview can be a formality if the organization has a fair, straightforward and understandable reward structure. Here the individuals know exactly where they stand and increments, merit awards and bonuses are virtually automatic according to some well-understood and clearly agreed set of rules. In organizations where the distribution of rewards is left largely to the individual departmental heads and managers, the reward review interview becomes a scene for bargaining. Heated discussion often takes place between members of staff and their manager. The reward review interview then becomes a critical interaction between managed and manager. Such interactions can be fraught with emotion and anxiety and, if handled badly, can cause members of staff considerable unhappiness. They are a danger to be avoided.

When entering such an interview, it is important to be aware of the individual's own expectations about the rewards that he hopes to receive. A manager should therefore enter a reward review interaction either fully aware of the individual's expectations, gained by observations and conversation over the previous review period, or by being prepared to sit down and discuss them, perhaps in considerable depth. If necessary the manager should be prepared to postpone announcing what reward he is going to recommend as a result of information gained and the discussion which has taken place at that particular time. It is thus suggested here that the reward review interview should be a flexible interaction, exploring and reviewing unexpected areas bearing on the needs of the individual.

Some research findings indicate that for some people financial and status rewards are really a source of anxiety rather than job satisfaction. They must be removed before concentrating on aspects of an individual's work experience which increase his commitment to his work. People do not see pay, status and other rewards in the same way. Pay is the all important motive for work for some people; for others it is far less so. Managers must therefore be aware of the tremendous range of individual differences amongst their staff in their attitudes to the kinds of rewards that the organization should be giving them. It is a common failing for managers to project their own needs upon their staff, thinking that what they value for themselves is also valued and wanted by their staff.

One of the main purposes of a reward review interview is for managers to make sure that they really understand the needs, values and expectations of the members of staff they are interviewing. That is usually the first section of the interview and, if they are known, can be short.

The purpose of the middle section is to discuss and build up to what the individual is likely to get by way of reward, or lack of it. If he is bursting to know, the joy or misery should not be delayed too long.

The final section of the interview is to ensure that the individual accepts the reward, the reasons for it, and, if possible, is happy with it. If the reward exceeds expectations there is no problem but, if it falls far short of expectations, the manager may have a grievance interview on his hands.

The process of reward reviews can perhaps best be understood by regarding it as a balancing activity. An organization must obtain work from its members in order to achieve profit or any other index of success. Individuals have needs for money, security and status which they hope will be satisfied by organizations employing them. Managers have organizational needs which they must achieve through their staff; they also want to meet their own standards of achievement, a quiet life or whatever special needs they have for themselves. These three groups of needs cannot all be met but they must be balanced. This should be the main outcome of an effective reward review procedure. However, a reward structure can only maintain a certain level of work and needs gratification by an organization. A function of a performance review is to improve on the existing levels of work performance and job satisfaction.

3
Potential reviews

The identification and communication of information about an individual's potential for different kinds and levels of work at some future date is probably the most technically difficult aspect of staff appraisal and development. It is also probably the most dangerous in possible psychological effects, for statements about an individual's potential, or lack of it, can be psychologically disturbing. There are also social problems, such as identifying 'crown princes': someone may have been labelled as heir-apparent and may start behaving in that role, even though he may not have the capacity for the work for which he is being groomed. There is also the 'self-fulfilling prophecy': making a prediction about a person's potential and publicly announcing it can bring about the prophecy.

The technical difficulty can be simply stated as to 'how, and with what kind of information, can one predict future human behaviour?'. This is the nub of a whole problem area of occupational psychology and has given psychologists cause for debate for many years. Nevertheless, attempts should be made to do this with people inside organizations, so that manpower planning can be carried out effectively. Therefore the requirement does exist to make judgements of a predictive kind about human behaviour. Organizations tend to establish a procedure which at least attempts to be more systematic in identifying potential and making use of this information rather than leaving things to chance. If any organization wants to work systematically in this field, it needs to establish a potential review procedure which should run parallel to, but still make use of, the information generated by the other kinds of reviews.

Objectives

The objectives of potential review procedures are identifying and making use of potential for different kinds of different levels of work in the organization. This potential is relative, in the sense that it is based on what individuals are doing at present in comparison with what their capacities and inclinations could allow them to do in the future.

Once potential has been identified the next objective is to realize it. This combines a discovery of whether or not the individuals are willing and interested in offering themselves for different kinds of work; also, are they ambitious enough to want to work at what is perhaps a significantly higher and more demanding level? This is followed by agreeing plans to realize this potential, through training courses, assignments and specially planned experience. Any potential review procedure should be aimed at fulfilling these objectives. It should therefore be seen not just as a labelling exercise, but as a scheme whereby individuals and an organization work together to make use of personal talents and aspirations to meet the long term needs of both.

Sources of information

The range and quality of information obtained about an individual's capacities and inclinations for work determines the effectiveness of any potential review. This information can be a mixture of objective data based on exact observations, leavened with subjective judgement based on fleeting clues or intuitive guesswork. Possible sources are listed below. It is important to note that by itself each and every type of information is inadequate. The whole point of a potential review is to assemble all the information and for decisions to be made on a comprehensive analysis of all the data available about the individual.

SELF REPORTS

Individuals' own assessment of their potential is clearly a necessary and relevant aspect of this procedure. The weakness of this information is that it is highly subjective. Some individuals are prone to overestimate their own ability, others to underestimate it. Although self-reported information is important, it is certainly not a sufficient source of data about potential.

Individuals are prone to confuse interest with ability. Interest in other kinds of work is not necessarily accompanied by ability to accomplish it. The converse also applies. Some people have the ability for certain kinds of work but do not wish to undertake it. It is often difficult for individuals to face the fact that they have not got what it takes for a certain kind of job, although they may urgently want to do it. It is a function of a potential review interview to help individuals come to terms with information from other sources about their abilities and interests, and the chances they may have of undertaking significantly higher level work.

IMMEDIATE MANAGER'S REPORTS

Similarly, an immediate manager may only have observed the individual in a narrow range of jobs. Such information may not necessarily be an indicator of high level performance. The fact that someone has failed or been successful in a lower level kind of job is relevant but not crucial. Studies have shown that a possible indicator of high level performance is a relative failure in a low level job. The well known 'Peter Principle' states that people who are only promoted on information based on their existing work performance will eventually reach a level of incompetence. Direct observation of performance in an existing job is an important but not complete way of identifying potential.

OBSERVATION BY SENIOR MANAGERS

Members of staff may come to the attention of managers very much senior to themselves. These senior managers sometimes pride themselves on their ability to pick out a young, relatively junior member of staff on the basis of a single report of outstanding performance, which is used as an indication of high level potential. This may well be useful information to accumulate; by itself it is not sufficient.

CONSULTANTS

The early identification of management potential has now become an important aspect of some management consultants' activities, especially in America. Assessment centres exist to

which staff can be sent for dispassionate and objective assessment of their capacities and inclinations for different kinds or
levels of work. These centres can be 'internal', staffed by
specially trained and qualified staff, or 'external' and run by
consultants or professional psychologists. Such centres make
use of various standardized tests of intelligence, thinking and
problem solving. Research is under way on the usefulness of
scored interest and inclination questionnaires. These 'pencil
and paper' scores are often combined with rated group exercises, 'simulated tasks' such as 'in-tray problems' and interviews. These have the advantage of being relatively objective
ways of assessing an individual and can perhaps provide the
most critical information on which to base an assessment of a
person's potential. This data may be precise but it is not likely
to be comprehensive. Long-term validity studies about such
predictors are scanty and the data must be interpreted with
care.

It can be concluded then that all types of information about
a person's past and present performance, and his yet unutilized
aptitudes, should be brought together within a potential review
procedure, so some kind of assembly documents are required.

Documentation

Frequently a potential review section appears on an organization's standard appraisal document. It is often immersed
amongst the current performance information, and can appear
as a global assessment about 'readiness for promotion' or
'suitability for responsibility'. Clearly some specially designed
form, with separate instructions on how to complete it, is
required. It would contain space for ratings, tests scores and
special isolated judgements, all accumulated on a single document. This should be so designed that the key information
stands out. In large organizations it should lend itself to
computer processing or other mechanical means whereby
underutilized knowledge, skills and aptitudes could be sig-
nalled to the organization. In particular the form should
distinguish between the abilities of the individual and his
interests. Separate sections on the form should differentiate
clearly between these two aspects. Another section should cover
relationships with people. Often capacity and inclination are

not enough for certain high level kinds of managerial work. Working with and through other people is frequently crucial. This area of human activity is often the most difficult to assess.

The structure and content of any staff appraisal form, as mentioned above, is a signalling device. For the use of the organization itself, it assembles information about the individuals making it up; it also signals to those individuals what the organization values. Thus the actual design of potential review documentation can be important in letting people know what it takes to be successful in a particular organization.

The use of some kind of graphic or multiple step rating scale, where a judgement about a person's behaviour, aptitude or trait is indicated by a mark along a scale, is frequently seen on appraisal forms. Such devices may appear to be exact or even 'scientific' ways of assessing people but they are fraught with technical dangers. Many problems surround the design and use of scales, such as:

halo effects: rating high or low on all scales to conform to a previous overall assessment

constant errors: being too lenient or too tough, or just always using the centre of the scale

multidimensionality: the scale attempts to measure many behaviours or attributes along one dimension

anchoring: how are points at the ends and along the scales to be defined?

relative or absolute: are the assessments to be based on absolute standards or in comparison with the standards that currently exist within the company?

scale length: how many points make up the scale and whether there should be an odd or even number of them.

All these effects, and others, make the use of scales a dangerous approach to recording assessments about people who are being appraised. But they have one important and useful contribution to make as a signalling rather than as a measuring device. If such scales are incorporated in a form they can be used to throw up data on those who have something extra to offer in comparison with their group. Care must of course be taken not to overlook people when using this process.

This form is best kept in some central management development/human resources office, where it can be analysed and summary reports made. A decision must then be made on the most appropriate person to discuss this summary data with the individual member of staff.

When using computerized records the Data Protection Act of 1984 must be kept in mind. Initially at least this Act stipulates that *opinions* about an individual are subject to access, whereas *intentions* are not. Thus any judgements, however soundly based, about an individual's potential are, if stored in computer files, subject to access. Management must therefore judge whether this is desirable having in mind that high indications of promotability will lead to disaffection if not fulfilled for any reason, or conversely, that a low rating may lead to diminution of commitment. Manual records are not affected by the Act.

The potential review interview

Who should carry out the potential review interview? Some organizations have a board made up of an individual's own immediate superiors and moderators from other departments, or even other organizations. Clearly this is an attempt to be fair, objective and balanced. But boards lend themselves to the criticism that can be levelled at all kinds of panel interview: that it is extremely difficult to establish rapport in a group interview. This is often the most ineffective and inappropriate way of discussing dispassionately an individual's needs, aspirations and views. However, panels do have advantages and can provide a useful final stage in any potential review procedure.

Potential review interviews are usually best carried out by some special officer designated by the organization to assemble the information and to discuss an individual's future with him. He should have available all the information on the potential review document; he should also have the authority to call for additional information. In the interview he should discuss quite dispassionately the man's own views on his potential and the accumulated assessments derived from information collected about him.

Such staff development departments can be a powerful force

in the organizational structure. If they are not properly controlled they can develop into faceless individuals who have the power to shift and move. Nobody really knows who they are and how they are directed themselves. This is a delicate area for organizational politics. Some organizations wisely do not risk establishing them. But if they can be integrated and monitored effectively, and staffed with competent human resources managers, they can contribute considerably to an organization's long-term growth.

There is an opportunity here to make use of long serving and experienced senior managers; they may be out of the political arena because they are in full command of important jobs which they have little inclination to change. Their particular kind of job enlargement could be the responsibility for monitoring the progress of a group of young managers. This role of mentor can give them a source of extra job satisfaction in applying their accumulated wisdom and managerial counselling skill. At the same time it provides a source of independent and detailed guidance for the younger member of staff. But senior managers will naturally need selecting and then careful training in the additional skills that potential reviews entail.

How much of the potential review assessment should be communicated to the individual and his manager? Some kind of summary of a person's potential clearly needs to be made. If it is given too wide a distribution it may lend itself to the weakness of self-fulfilling prophecies, or black marks on the record, which can hinder rather than help a person's development. Consequently reports in general rather than specific terms are the most defensible. There is always the problem of borderline cases. Organizations which attempt to label people too precisely as A, B, C or D performers to signify their speed and range of development, sometimes give themselves difficulty in marginal cases. This is an area which has to be treated with extreme delicacy and there can be no hard and fast rules as to how it should be done.

There are some advantages in identifying the more able members of staff and attempting to bring them along quickly. A 'management pool' can be created which can act as a motivating force on individuals to move into the demanding areas of work and so become noticed as high flyers. But the existence of such a group of staff could also have a damaging influence on the inclination to work hard amongst marginal performers. If an organization wishes to emphasize high level performance, and is so managed that high level performance can be used, that is a defensible procedure. If the work to be done in the organization is so constrained and inflexible that there is not much scope for high level performance, it is probably better not to publish or release any signals as to a person's potential. In the long run this could only cause unhappiness by raising expectations which are not subsequently met.

Gaining acceptance for a potential review procedure depends mainly on whether or not organizations are willing to use the information that such a procedure generates. It must be seen as a technically sound procedure, based on as much objective information as can be made available. This is why some organizations go to the expense of employing outside consultants to do this work on their behalf. It is difficult to train lay managers to spot potential; it is hard enough for a professional psychologist to do so using all the available techniques over two or three days of special tests and exercises. As long as an organization attempts systematically to accumulate, sift and balance all sources and types of information, it is on the way to having an effective potential spotting scheme. But it is misguided if it thinks that looking through 'magic-glasses' or feeding 'royal-jelly' to the chosen few is sufficient to identify and release management potential.

4
Performance reviews

Improving the performance of people in their existing jobs should be the principal aim of any active staff appraisal scheme. People go into an organization with something between the minimum and optimum amount of capacity and inclination to perform their appointed jobs. They then, whilst in service with the organization, frequently undergo experiences which reduce the inclination to apply these capacities. A passive staff appraisal scheme maintains the initial level of ability and interest for the work to be done, whereas by definition any active scheme *adds* to people's capacity and inclination to work. This is the kernel of staff appraisal. Consequently, helping staff to get better at their jobs is an important part of the work of managers in their day to day interactions with their staff. One of the features of an effective manager is the way in which he allocates time, and how well he conducts his reviews of the performances of his staff. It can be argued that the most important part of every manager's job is to develop his own staff. If every manager is doing this, the organization cannot fail to become more effective. Perhaps these are the ground roots of all organizational development procedures and an essential accompaniment to any pruning or shaping of the organizational structure.

The first practical issue to consider is the frequency of the formal interview in performance reviews. In a highly stable, rigid organization once a year may be sufficient. For some members who have been doing the same job and who expect to be doing the same job in exactly the same way for more time to come, once a year may well be enough. For most members of staff more frequent reviews of their performance would be desirable, not just to let them know where they stand but also to give them feedback on their strengths and weaknesses and so help them improve their performance. Timing the frequency of such interviews is an important aspect of the judgement involved in performance review. For the young, able and energetic members of staff who have perhaps recently joined the organization, a performance review interview may be required weekly, if not daily in some circumstances. The best guide to frequency is based on the judgement of the manager as to how much change in behaviour can be achieved with that member of staff at that particular time. Too frequent reviews may make the individual feel that he is not trusted and that the manager is 'always in my hair'. Too infrequent reviews may lead to feelings of insecurity, anxiety and of 'being ignored'. This is a delicate balance of timing that a manager must decide upon for each individual member of staff.

Objectives

A performance review procedure must result in either or both of the following:

A DEVELOPMENT STEP

An increase in the capacity to work of the member of staff. This can be either an increase in knowledge, a change in attitude or an extension of skill and can result from the review or from some experience or training which has been agreed during the course of the review. This increase in capacity can be defined as the *development step*. It derives from the assertion that at any given moment there is an aspect of knowledge, skill or a change in attitude that any worker could acquire which would make him better at his job. The main purpose of observing an individual at work is to identify just what this piece of knowledge, skill or attitude could be. Once identified, this is the next development step for that individual. If an individual worker can be encouraged to take this step, the assumption is that he would then become better at the job. It is therefore the major task of a manager, when observing or considering the work of his staff, to identify for each one just what this development step could be.

It is then the function of the performance review interview first to check whether or not this development step, as assumed by the manager, is realistic and if so how it can be brought about.

The second main objective of a performance review is to bring about an increase in inclination to work. As a result of the review any blockages, brakes or other sources of frustration detracting from the individual worker's performance are noticed and removed or their effects are lessened. In addition the needs and expectations of members of staff are observed. Arrangements are made for these to be met as far as possible, so that an increase in the inclination to work is achieved. This objective can be called motivation growth. Once again the assumption is that there is either something standing psychologically in the way of an individual member of staff's increased performance or some need or expectation which, if met, would make that individual more satisfied with his job and want to work harder at it. It must be emphasized that motivation only occurs when a need is met; it is *derivative* rather than causative. Diagnosing a person's next need and devising an action plan that *increases the chances* of meeting it is the basis of all motivation growth.

It may be argued that the performance review is also an occasion for punishment, where the individual's misdemeanors may be noted and subsequently pointed out to him. The assumption is that, once a person knows about his errors, he will not repeat them, will be reasonably contrite and so become a more effective employee. Punitive interviews may sometimes be necessary and can be defended on the ground that reviewing such misdemeanors will result in an overall increase in performance. But punishment does not necessarily bring about an increase in capacity or a growth in inclination to work. The chances are that it may do just the opposite, so any punitive content to performance reviews should be the exception rather than the rule. If some kind of punishment is thought necessary a sharp reprimand at the time of the misdemeanor should suffice and then be forgotten. It should only enter the performance review procedure if the individual has not improved as a result; the case then becomes a problem to be solved by discussion, training or more drastic means.

Sources of information

The main sources of information about a person's performance at the job are the person and the immediate manager. Self-appraisal is being increasingly used as a basis for staff development schemes. The underlying idea is that if an individual can be encouraged to work out for himself what he should be doing differently, so that he can get better at his job, much of the immediate manager's task is eased. But there is a real limitation to the amount of self development any individual can achieve. Few people can objectively analyse their own strengths and weaknesses and make realistic plans to do something about them. For some, self-analysis can lead to inaccurate conclusions. It then becomes doubly difficult for the manager to shift an individual away from an apparent perceived strength or weakness, and to help that individual to gain insight into areas where changes in behaviour may be more relevant to the immediate job demands. However, the process of encouraging an individual to start by looking at himself is clearly a valuable way into an active staff development scheme, not least because of the long term benefit it can bring.

The information from the individual and the immediate manager can be supplemented by reports from colleagues, customers and other people with whom he comes in contact during the course of his work. All this information must be realistically assessed as there is considerable scope for bias and inaccuracy. Human observation is highly subjective. Illusion and delusion are normal everyday aspects of human perception.

Two problems need to be faced by a manager using these sources of information: how to control bias and false data and how to handle the sheer volume of information available. To tackle these problems, organizations resort to designing a special performance review form. This is discussed below.

Documentation

In theory no special kind of form is required for undertaking performance reviews. A blank sheet of paper is perhaps all that is required by a thorough and precise observer of human behaviour. Many managers keep a sheet of paper, a card or a page in a notebook on which to record observations and notes about the performance of each member of staff. This is a haphazard and chancy way to build up relevant information and therefore, unless the manager is particularly skilled at reviewing performance, it should not be considered sufficient.

The first level of elaboration beyond blank sheets of paper is to define the kinds of observations that are recorded. Guidelines can be laid down on the critical and key aspects of the job, or what kinds of performance are significantly above or below what is regarded as standard, and only observations of that kind recorded. This approach derives from the ideas behind such procedures as 'management by exception', 'management by objectives' and more broadly the 'critical incidents technique'. It has the virtue of tackling the problem of which information to observe and record. The difficulty is to decide what is critical. If considerable care is not taken, both key features of a praiseworthy performance, particularly of an innovative or collaborative kind, and unco-operative and underhand behaviour may pass unnoticed.

Many organizations consequently design an appraisal form which provides a guide to help the manager to make relevant observations; it provides sets of questions to help him to be objective and balanced in his assessments. This is done through adjective checklists, forced choice questions, employee comparison scales and sometimes rating scales as described in the potential review section. These forms are often seen as the cornerstone of staff appraisal and development schemes.

The design and development of these forms is fraught with problems. The final form more often reflects the background and training of the designer than the needs of an organization. It also frequently signals the organization's value structure and personnel philosophy rather than real behaviour standards and policy. Detailed examination of the form will easily indicate whether it was designed by a committee: this can be seen from a mixture of styles, intentions and compromises. If an engineer/mathematician or historian/philosopher has been mainly responsible for the design, this usually shows through attempts by the former to introduce precise measuring devices, and by the latter to introduce elegant descriptive categories.

The most common failing of such a form is its attempt to include everything about staff appraisal and development in a single document. Evaluation, potential, current performance and training needs are often all under scrutiny, usually at the expense of each individual category. It is not possible to give detailed guidelines on how to design a form. There are no model forms which would suit the needs of all organizations at all stages of their development. However, four clear principles emerge at the design stage: keep it simple; don't attempt too much; observe and record behaviour rather than personality; build in capacity for change and development. As long as the form is acceptable to both the appraisers and the appraised it is likely to perform its main function: to provide the basis for an effective performance review interview. It might be useful to refer to the IPM publication *Personnel Administration Made Simple* which provides examples of forms used for good company practice.

The performance review interview

The main concern here is the quality of the relationship between the manager and the member of staff being appraised. If the relationship is a good one, managers will not have a great deal of difficulty communicating with and improving the performance of their staff. Unfortunately most managers think that the relationship between them and their staff is better than it actually is. If relationships are poor, managers must make improvement their first objective. If they succeed, performance review interviews will follow smoothly and effectively; if they fail the interviews will always be rough and the direct objective of increased performance difficult to obtain.

The place of the performance review interview is important. The obvious place, the manager's own office, is not necessarily best. As a guideline, the more formal the purpose of the interview the more formal the setting should be. Sometimes a performance can be discussed and an improvement gained through words exchanged whilst passing in the corridor, or on other even less formal occasions. Once again judgement is required.

Just before starting a performance review interview, a manager should sit quietly and plan what exactly he hopes to achieve as a result of the forthcoming interaction: he should decide what objectives he can achieve with this particular individual at this particular time. But it must be stressed that, like all good plans, they should be dropped if subsequent information indicates that the assumptions behind the plan are erroneous.

Preparation is equally as important for the subject of the review. Being called unexpectedly into a manager's office for a performance review is unlikely to contribute to success. Giving an opportunity to prepare, or even providing help in preparing for the review will usually make it constructive. It should not be forgotten that both participants want the interview to go well even if they do hold different viewpoints. Both will have things they want to say which may require careful thought beforehand.

Strategies

The strategy for the interaction must be decided next. There are various types of approaches to performance review interviewing; the interviewer must choose the one most appropriate to his plan and subject. It must be stressed that there is 'no one best way' to conduct a performance review interview. If there were, the whole activity would be a manipulative operation rather than a complex human skill.

If the basic assumption is made that a manager never has enough information, either about the individual's previous performances during the review period or about his own thoughts and feelings on the individual's performance, the first stage of a performance review interview is to check and collect information. After any opening generalities this information usually bears upon a particular problem of performance, either one of capacity or inclination. If this is so it can be argued that the way to approach a performance review interview is through a particular problem thrown up during the previous review period. The interview therefore progresses and this particular problem is raised by one of the parties. This strategy, known as the *problem solving* approach, can be regarded as the base for all other approaches and the variations depend on the basic capacities, inclinations and needs of the member of staff being appraised.

If the individual is well aware of the problem hampering his improved performance, and even perhaps of the possible solutions; if he is clearly willing and able to do something about it himself (and if in the judgement of the interviewer something can be done) all that is requested is to set some target or goal for that individual. This can be called the *goal setting* approach. This goal, objective or target setting approach is particularly applicable to the young and able who are on top of their jobs and going places. This can be a short and purposeful interview. The manager merely has to agree on a realistic and attainable target or standard which the subject will reach in a certain period. A whole series of targets can of course be established with the individual at any one performance review interview if, in the judgement of the manager, the subject is capable of attaining them.

The next variation is applicable to those members of staff who, although they may well be capable of a development step, may not be too willing to undertake it. They may be awkward, self-opinioned or difficult in other ways. The interaction for these people is one of telling the individual what the problem is, spelling it out as precisely as possible using the evidence to hand, and then selling them the solution. This is the *tell-sell* type. This approach appears authoritarian and stresses that the manager knows best. It is common particularly when a senior and perhaps elderly manager interacts with a young, relatively junior and inexperienced member of staff. These interviews can be short, sharp and purposeful. The trouble is that the strategy may not gain the commitment of the individual. The subject may leave the interview with apparent agreement to do what the boss says but not really believing that this should be done.

The next approach is with a member of staff who needs to be told what to do but is also full of his own ideas, some of which may well be relevant to the problems that have been experienced. This person may however lack either self-confidence or the ability to choose a course of action. The strategy here is the *tell-listen* approach. The manager describes his own observations and thoughts about the subject's performance and then waits until the individual has suggested the line of action which the manager has previously decided upon as being a real solution to the problem. The manager then directs the discussions to settle on this line of action and encourages the individual to suggest how it can be accomplished. The listening component of this interview is therefore important. Its advantage is that, if the individual does suggest for himself what he should do, he is far more likely to be committed to the action than that which is sold to him under the more authoritarian style.

The next approach is even more permissive. It is much more applicable in situations where the subject is suffering frustration, alienation or conflict. It is therefore a problem of inclination, maintenance or growth rather than capacity development. It is the strategy to use when the problem raised by the manager unleashes a stream of complaints. It is also applicable to situations where nothing can be done about the problem except to chip away at it as best one can. In these circumstances the *listen-support* style of interviewing is the appropriate one. What the manager has to do is listen to what the subject has to say and nod, signifying that he has at least heard what has been said though not necessarily agreeing. This is akin to talking out a problem. If the interaction develops in this way, the manager must let it go as long as the subject needs to talk.

This style of interviewing is often called 'non-directive' or even 'counselling'. It can be time consuming but, when the situation demands it, it is essential that the manager should drop all the other problems which he may have had in mind simply to discuss and clear the ground. It is unrealistic to think that an employee will change his ways, and will attempt to learn something or acquire a new skill or even change his attitude, if he has strong feelings about certain problems which he and his manager are experiencing. If he talks himself through this problem, and it is apparent that he is being understood, he usually feels much better about his work. The manager can then bring the interview round again to the particular problems he has identified and which now need to be resolved. This is a kind of psychological contract: the manager indicates he is willing to listen to all problems put forward by the subject and, in return, the subject listens to the performance problems which the manager himself wishes to raise. These can be difficult interviews to conduct but, when they arise, they are vital to certain kinds of staff relationship problems.

A performance review interview consists of three stages: first, the opening where the interviewer checks over his observations, opinions and points and compares them with the subject's own account of his performance over the review period. This is the data-gathering, data-checking stage of the interview.

The middle stage of the interview is the attempt to achieve both a development step and motivation growth through using the appropriate interview strategy.

The final stage of the interview is to sum up, agree conclusions and plan the next step. Whenever possible the interview should finish in a tidy and purposeful way. The individual should understand exactly where he now stands and what he has to do. Similarly, the manager must end with a clearer idea of the capacities and inclinations of the individual and what he is expecting the individual to achieve in as precise terms as possible, over the forthcoming review period. This is the stage at which notes can most appropriately be taken. Note taking can help to clarify the results of the interview and focus attention on major points which have evolved. If the interview has been a particularly emotional or strenuous one, it is probably not appropriate to take notes but perhaps simply to note the date of the next interview.

Once the subject has left the room, detailed notes of what has transpired can well be made to help the manager's memory. These can be considered the next time the interviewer is planning a performance review with this particular member of staff.

At this point questions concerning the formal aspects of a staff appraisal system can become obtrusive. This book has stressed the importance of reaching mutually agreed action plans rather than reporting officially on staff performance. With this as the main objective, the 'reporting' and 'evaluation' components of staff appraisal are unimportant. However, because of previous experiences of individuals and the social history of the organization, the reporting/evaluation aspect may still be seen to be the main purpose of the staff appraisal system, despite policy proclamations to the contrary. This is counter-productive, because such beliefs can hinder the sharing of information and the gaining of commitment. If such suspicions exist then the organization should question the need for automatic form-filling, for countersigning and for sending in reports. As has been indicated above, the only report that needs be 'sent in' is the fact that a meeting has taken place, and even this is not essential. If sensitivities and mistrust exist this may be the most that can be agreed. It is to be stressed that there is no real need for a formal report at all in developmental approaches to staff appraisal. However, if either the manager or the managed insists that a report of the performance review is sent in (usually for disciplinary or grievance reasons) then the 'system' should allow for this to happen. In these circumstances a counter-signature would at least indicate that both participants in the interview are aware of each other's position. But such interviews are hopefully rare in organizations, and it must be regarded as poor personnel management practice to design a whole system around undesirable events. Any system must be planned to be supportive of skilful management activity; if it gets in the way or complicates relationships, then its use should be questioned. The theme of this book is that staff appraisal systems should be the means, not the end, of active staff development.

Questions and statements

It may be useful to consider the detailed construction of a performance review interview. Any purposeful interaction or interview consists mainly of a series of questions and statements by each of the participants. Whilst one is questioning or stating, the other should be listening. There is no doubt that the quality of each activity is enormously important to the overall quality of the interview. How well the interviewer constructs the questions, how relevant and appropriate the statements are and how well the interviewer listens to what the subject is saying are all essential aspects of the skill of appraisal interviewing. However, each of these activities should bear upon the wider purposes of bringing about a development step or motivation growth. The ultimate purpose is to gain commitment to whatever attempt at a change in capacity or inclination has been agreed to in the interview. Consequently the quality of questions, statements and listening should be judged in relation to those objectives.

QUESTIONS

There are various kinds of questions. The most usual in any interview are open questions. *Open* questions begin with words like, 'tell me about', 'how about', and 'will you go into and describe to me'. *Closed* questions usually begin with words like 'how many', 'how often', 'did you ever'. Clearly a balance is required between these two types. If there are too many open questions the interview sounds inconsequential and flabby. Too many closed questions make the interview sound like an interrogation.

Questions which are not very helpful and which usually result from the interviewer trying too hard or putting his own point of view, are *leading* questions. These begin with the phrase 'you do' or generally 'have you not?' Perhaps most questions beginning with the word 'you' invariably lead to the answer that the interviewer is expecting. Another unhelpful type is the *multiple* question, which is really a series of questions run together in such a way that the subject does not know which one to answer. Multiple questions also allow the subject to answer only that part which suits him best. Such questions are usually signs of weakness of technique or inexperience in the interviewer and can be trained out easily.

STATEMENTS

Rhetorical questions are usually obvious, ie those with an exclamation mark rather than question mark, which tell the subject what the interviewer believes. These may have a use. They will at least tell the subject where he stands but if a statement is actually incorrect it can readily lead to an argument between the interviewer and interviewee.

Once an argument develops in an interview little is usually achieved by either side. It is easy for the interviewer to display scorn, destructive criticism or displeasure. Such statements may have their use but they must be guarded against. Unless they help the overall purpose, they are a waste of time and can endanger the relationship that exists.

Listening is perhaps most difficult for senior and experienced managers to do well. Many managers are so used to giving instructions and directives that they fall out of the habit, or lose the skill, of listening to what people are saying to them. This may be a useful way to save time in day to day interactions with members of staff. But an interviewer who does not listen to what the subject has to say immediately destroys the quality of the communication which can be established. This is why sufficient time should be set aside so that the manager does not feel rushed. The manager should have prevented all possible interruptions and attempted to create an air of 'timeless calm'. The simple fact that the interviewer is listening can have an enormously therapeutic effect upon the anxieties and aspirations of a member of staff. When asked to assess the quality of an interview that they have just experienced, staff are sometimes heard to say 'he did at least listen to me'. In some authoritarian organizations where little listening takes place, the effect on staff can be extremely beneficial.

Listening also has the advantage of giving the interviewer thinking time. He is able to consider what the subject has just told him. He can assess its relevance to the problems that he himself has identified and he can perhaps assess its significance to the needs and aspirations of the person who is talking. He can use listening time too to spot any danger signals from the subject, and so have greater control over the emotional content of the interaction. He can also use it to assess the impact he is having on the subject and whether or not he is achieving his own objectives. So interjections of the kind 'go on', 'tell me more', 'go into that in more detail', said in a thoughtful and encouraging way, are essential aspects of the detailed content of a performance review interview.

Special cases

The above comments are relevant for a wide range of staff. The mid-range of performers particularly would profit from the systematic approach to performance improvement that the procedure involves. Where the technique falls short is with the extremes amongst members of staff.

One extreme group comprises those able people who feel that their capacities are being persistently under-utilized and their inclinations deliberately disregarded. Their sense of grievance is so strong that they may be on the brink of resigning. Their performance review is dominated by these feelings, their standard of work is deteriorating rather than improving and they need to be heard through a *grievance interview*.

Such interviews differ from those already described in two important ways. The first is in the proportion of time taken up by interviewer and subject. Most effective interviews would average about 50 per cent each, tending towards 40 per cent interviewer talking and 60 per cent interviewee in the more skilled and purposeful interactions. In the grievance interview the subject would be talking for nearer 80–90 per cent of the time. This would be achieved through the kind of questions used; in particular the interviewer would use *reflective questions*. Rather than directing the course of the discussion by seeking specific information, the interviewer would encourage the member of staff to talk out his grievance by reflecting each statement that he makes back to him. Slowly the foundations and structures of the grievance will emerge, if possible to be understood and action agreed and started to dismantle it.

At the other extreme, the member of staff is so lacking in capacity and inclination for his job, and so resistant to all efforts at achieving any development step or motivation growth that the objective becomes a *separation interview*. In its most callous form it sounds like a 'tell-tale' interaction. To be both humane and effective it should be a mixture of all the approaches described above, with a balance of telling-selling-listening-supporting and finally goal setting, when the terms and timing of the separation are agreed. Needless to say, all separation interviews must follow the code of practice.

Follow-up and self-assessment

After every interview or batch of interviews, the interviewer should ask himself how well he did: how well did he achieve his objectives? what he himself learnt from the discussions and in what ways he could become better at carrying out interviews? As has been stressed, interviewing is a skill. The only way to improve a skill is to practise with some kind of feedback about how well the act achieved its target.

In part II examples are given of training interviewers by means of feedback given by observers and tutors. In the field, this kind of feedback is not usually possible. The feedback which is available is that from the interviewer himself. Therefore if the manager wants to improve his appraisal interviewing, he must ask himself after each interview how well he did, what he should have done differently and what he will do next time. Interviewing is a limitless skill in the sense that one can always get better at it, no matter at what particular level one is at the moment.

45

A useful additional strategy is to risk asking one's subject how well the interview has met that subject's own particular needs and aspirations. It needs strong-minded managers actually to invite assessment from their staff. This can however be extremely rewarding to both, in giving some positive feedback about performance to the interviewer and in strengthening the relationships between managers and their staff. In this way the foundations can be laid for a better interview later on. The quality of the relationship which exists between managers and their staff is perhaps the most important single factor which determines the success of appraisal interviews. If this is poor, no matter how well the interviewer constructs his questions and statements, the quality of the performance review interview is also likely to be poor. Similarly if the relationships between managers and their staff are excellent, it would take a very badly constructed performance review to undermine it. Most managerial relationships in industry and commerce vary between these two extremes. It is the main objective of interview training to increase the chances of a performance review interview being effective in improving performance at work.

Training for performance review skills

Any attempts to improve a staff appraisal and development procedure could start at the point of attempting to improve managers' skills at performance review interviewing. The alternative is to revise the paperwork. This approach can take a long time before benefits begin to show. Even then the system could be technically inadequate or socially unacceptable, or both. Starting by training the managers has the advantage that the new procedure could then be evolved through them rather than imposed upon them. Once they become aware of the basic principles and skilled in applying them, a staff appraisal and development system which really works can be built up by the organization. In the meantime managers have been helped in their task of managing their staff and employees have been managed more effectively. All have therefore gained.

The second part of this book describes how one organization applied some of these basic principles, and the results so far obtained by improving staff appraisal through training.

Part II
Improving
staff appraisal
through training

5
Introduction

Most books on staff appraisal end here, with the description of exactly what the process is seen to be.

Some of these books do go on to ask the question 'How does an organization commence a staff appraisal programme?, and invariably conclude 'at the top'. Some go into considerable detail about the design of the appraisal forms and the problems of gaining acceptance for them, and perhaps, say that some kind of training will be required to facilitate their use. Very few texts attempt to be explicit about the actual behaviour of managers that would lead to staff being better at their jobs. The assumption that is widely prevalent is that all an organization should do is to admit to the need for staff development, agree what it is, say it should happen, design a system and then wait for the results. As in all areas of knowledge the gap between a concept and its application is enormous, particularly in the area of management development.

At the very beginning of collaboration between 'industry' and 'university' that led to this book the first question raised was *how* should staff appraisal be carried out? The decision had already been taken that whatever was decided would require training, so what was the behaviour required of the managers that would lead to an effective staff appraisal procedure?

The original courses to train managers in the concepts provided the opportunity to observe directly role-played staff appraisal interviews and provided material, audio and video tapes and questionnaires completed by interviewees, observers and tutors, to be studied in depth. As this material accumulated it became clear that existing concepts to explain the process, and contemporary techniques of staff appraisal, were not sufficient to establish an effective approach to changing people's behaviour at work.

Resulting from this continuous analysis and modification the training changed from *course* to *workshop* with all that this implies. No longer was it prescriptive, working *on* people to precise standards; instead it became an occasion when skilled tutors worked *with* members to develop their own style and extract the maximum benefit from the intensive contact with tutors and fellow managers.

It is very clear now that the activity is a very high level skill. The first conceptual analysis produced a block diagram (see figure 2 opposite) of 11 interacting sections. This has developed into a tree-chart containing 20 'branches' and 170 'leaves', too large to publish here. Such a conceptual analysis is not necessary for 'learners' of the skill to understand, but it at least provides 'tutors' with an awareness of the components and complexity of the skill. The block diagram raises two issues. The first concerns the structure of the process. The approach taken here is that it is a *dynamic* rather than *sequential* activity. As each stage emerges, it can have effects both forwards and backwards within any particular interview, the interviewer being adaptive. A skilled interview grows and adapts in accordance with the information that emerges within it. Unfortunately, many interviewers are trained to proceed in a sequential, step-wise fashion, the interview being regarded then as an operation rather than a skill. The next issue is what to call the interaction between the manager and the member of staff. The common term is *staff appraisal interview*. Earlier in this book it was called the *performance review interview*. All these terms have unfortunate connotations and many attempts have been made to find a suitable descriptive term. The one suggested here is *'work review and action plan'* (WRAP); but this term is still to obtain wide acceptance. The policy followed is to use the term within a particular organization that reflects the culture and the intention for the procedure that will have the minimum resistance to its use.

The bridge between the concepts of active staff development and its practice, ie the *what* and the *how*, is spanned by training. Over the years, as the complexity of the skill has emerged, and the level of competance of the managers has increased, so the training has become more sophisticated. The original principles and structure, both of which have changed remarkably little are set out in the subsequent chapters.

Figure 2

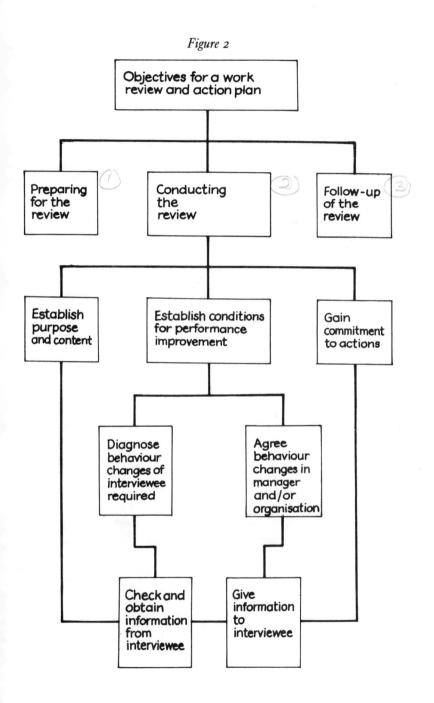

6

The training needs

In describing the design of the training programme it is first necessary to look back at the events which brought it about. The collaboration between industry and university, from which this training approach developed, first took place at Fisons plc. Companies' problems may differ but there should always be a common starting point for the successful introduction of such programmes: commitment from the top. This was certainly evident at Fisons plc.

Introduction to the case study

No doubt in common with many companies, Fisons was becoming increasingly disturbed by the difficulties experienced in ensuring that its managers carried out proper performance review interviews with their staff.

Early manifestations of this appeared at the time of the annual salary review when certain managers, although happy to advise staff personally that their salary was to be increased, apparently shrank from an interview when no increase or even a minor one was to be awarded. Some were advising employees that they had now reached the top of their scale. Since in most cases this was the first inkling the subjects had had, it was not surprising that lack of opportunity to discuss progress had become a matter of some discontent. Staff who were not able to discuss their progress could not know what to do to improve it. Rigorous action was taken to correct this situation and each manager was required to certify that he had interviewed each of his employees personally at the time that their salary was reviewed.

Later the company employed consultants to advise upon the whole of its salary structure and administration as part of a complete reconstruction of its personnel policy. Their report indicated that insufficient time was being given to performance assessment and improvement. Many managers reported that they were uncomfortable in the interview situation and unsure of what was expected of them. This lack of skill had been confirmed by the training department, where managers attending courses on selection interviewing were asking for advice on how to conduct performance review interviews.

Performance assessment would be a vital factor in the success of the new salary scheme as it would play an important part in the individual's salary progression. In addition, there were also clear practical implications for the individual's career development and effectiveness. The introduction of this scheme was considered an appropriate time for the group's training department to set up a major programme of training in the staff appraisal area which received full commitment from its top management.

Surveying the training needs

It became obvious early on to the training group concerned that, although we knew the organization's objectives and policy about staff appraisal, we needed to know more about actual standards of appraisal in the field. A survey would show more precisely what training was needed and what standards should be set. Although procedures and forms differed between divisions there was a common factor in that all Fisons managers were required to carry out appraisal interviews.

A request for training came from a divisional sales department. That particular department already conducted appraisals of representatives and sales management twice a year, using a form which set out in detail the qualities and standards required. Rating was done on a five point scale. Those with knowledge of each specific manager made informal adjustments to the ratings to compensate for known bias.

We set out to sample about 10 per cent of the representatives and sales management to find out how well the interviews went, where they were conducted, how much warning subjects had of an impending interview, any weaknesses known to the appraiser, what weaknesses were apparent to the subject and any effects on both managers and subordinates.

An additional objective of this study was to gather material which would provide basic incidents for incorporation in case studies to be written for use in a training course.

The physical environment of the interview varied widely. Few managers conducted an 'across the table' interview. Many held it side by side to reduce formality, often because the interview took place in a car, usually in a car park or down a quiet lane. Some interviews took place in lounge bars, or over lunch and occasionally in the subordinate's home.

As would be expected, conducting interviews in a public place seemed to be inhibiting for the subject.

In general there seemed to be a lack of appreciation of the advantages of a business like environment for the interview.

Many managers commented that the training they had received in selection interviewing heightened their awareness of the need for effective tactics in other interview situations. However, they felt unable to adapt selection interviewing skills to the appraisal situation.

Managers appeared to have a reasonably consistent approach to their assessment of performance and potential but they differed widely in ratings and in their method of conducting the appraisal interview. Some managers never showed the appraisal form to the appraised, others showed it before completion; some showed ratings only, others showed the completed appraisal. Exposing the form was generally used as a means of promoting discussion.

Some managers informed the appraised of the impending interview and others did not. Some sent a blank appraisal form asking the subject to rate himself; others discussed the appraisal in general terms only; and others saw it as an opportunity for a detailed and lengthy discussion.

A few managers confessed to difficulty in opening up subjects for discussion, particularly aspects concerned with a person's dress, habits or acceptability. One manager described how it took six stops in front of a tailor's window before it dawned on his subordinate that he should alter his style of dress. Most subjects would have welcomed more directness from their managers. One commented 'it was some days before I realized what he was getting at, he was so indirect...'

Many subordinates would have welcomed the opportunity of having a senior manager present during the interview to ensure that their relationship with their manager did not prevent a complete and fair assessment of job circumstances and potential. Managers on the other hand felt that such a situation would spoil rapport and unbalance the interview in management's favour.

At the time it was outside the terms of reference of the training department to redesign the staff appraisal procedures that existed within the group. From the point of view of the trainers the prime need was for improvement in interview technique. No matter what procedures and forms existed each manager still had the task of communicating the result of his appraisal to each member of his staff.

Three further points emerged:

1 There were shortcomings in assessing what motivated a particular man and gained his commitment. Managers also had difficulties in interpreting the factors which contributed to his overall performance such as intelligence, life goals, domestic circumstances, personality traits etc.
2 These difficulties were heightened by an inability to pursue such points systematically in an interview and by manager's unfamiliarity with this difficult field of human relations.
3 Many managers were able to make reasonable assessment of performance and identify areas of concern. Generally they stopped short of this and did not agree firm recommendations or actions where a man might improve.

We drew the overall conclusion that the major training need was to help managers improve the performance of staff in their existing jobs. We therefore decided to concentrate upon improving skill in conducting the performance review interview.

7
Designing the training

It was necessary now to decide the format of the course and its aims and objectives, taking account of the survey and applying the methods most suited to the organization.

The stated objectives were to improve understanding of the basis of objective appraisal and to practice and consolidate performance review interviewing skills. For the purpose of the training we defined a performance review as the skilled process by which a manager examines a subordinate's progress with him with the object of maintaining and improving the individual's effectiveness in his present job.

Included in the existing training programme was a course in selection interviewing techniques. It was structured on the basis of a workshop where members could practise on candidates. Members each conducted interviews within a group consisting of a tutor and two or three fellow members, who subsequently analysed and discussed the interview. This method had been extremely successful and managers found that analysis by their peers was particularly advantageous.

It therefore seemed natural to try to adapt this particular formula to the appraisal situation.

Course format

Only two days could be allocated to the course. We had therefore to compromise between the amount of time needed for practical training and analysis of interviewing performance, and the useful background 'education' we could provide on the theory of appraisal, the general techniques of interviewing and the 'applied psychology' elements, such as motivation, which could best be covered by a psychologist. The programme which emerged appears in appendix A on page

113. There are two practice sessions, each preceded by preparation sessions under tutorial guidance, and each followed by detailed analysis. There is adequate provision for the main theoretical elements to be covered.

Before writing the material for the practice sessions we first agreed a set of objectives for the exercises and then set the broad parameters of the job histories to be described. These were:

1 To provide background material for the interviewer and subject to conduct a simulated performance review interview, which would be realistic and revealing to the interviewer in terms of his choice of style and how he was perceived by the subject.
2 To provide the opportunity for interviewers to practice and apply lessons learned in earlier exercises.
3 To demonstrate to interviewers that in every appraisal situation there are two points of view, that of the interviewer and that of the subject; to show that often the interview is completed with very little of the subject's point of view being revealed.

Case histories

The most difficult part of the design of a course such as this is the construction of the practical interviewing material. There seem to be three ways to approaching the problem. One way is to provide the subject with a detailed fictitious recent job history and a structured pattern of responses to the interviewer's approach. A second is to have the interviewer examine the subject's recent job history with him. Yet another method is to provide only the outlines of job history, based on critical incidents, and to encourage the subject to colour his responses with his own job history, his feelings about his work and his natural reaction to the interviewer's approach. If a question irritates him, he should allow this to influence his reaction; if he feels he is being browbeaten he should react according to his own natural feelings about such treatment. This is more difficult for the subject as he has to try to give a true response whilst bearing in mind how he would be likely to behave if the interview were real and could have an effect on his career.

The first method has the advantage of enabling the designer to build teaching points into the practical material. It is possible to structure the material so that all interviewers come across these points and experience the same lessons. In other words the lessons learned are very much under the control of the designer, and therefore of the tutor.

The method has a number of disadvantages. First, it demands acting skill of the subject as he is acting out a predetermined role. Secondly, the brief he works to, which is almost as constraining as a script, often produces an unreal, stilted response which enhances the artificiality of the situation and usually inhibits the interviewer. The third and most serious disadvantage is that, because the response is predetermined, it is often not perceived by an interviewer as anything more than an illustration of the point of view of the tutor, ie a point of view he does not necessarily accept. For example, one typical behaviour pattern for managers appraising subordinates is to begin the interview with a list of poor or inadequate performance items for the period under review, often relating these to previous periods of poor performance. A typical reaction pattern on the part of the subject is to become defensive, to excuse himself, maybe to blame others, the manager himself or 'the system', and to feel resentment that his failures have received treatment first without reference to his successes. This inhibits any tendency for either party to examine the effects of the failures, how they came about and how to avoid them in the future. It usually prevents the subject from realizing deep within himself what his failures have been, what caused them and where he went wrong. He is far less likely to accept the interviewer's explanation than he is his own realization. Yet not all managers realize this and often they will not accept this interpretation from a tutor. They need to be convinced. They are unlikely to be convinced, however, if the point is merely illustrated and not brought out as a real feeling on the part of the subject.

The second method adds realism and requires little in the way of preparation. However, there are a number of grave disadvantages to the artificial relationship between interviewer and subject. It is one thing to expect a subject to be frank and constructive in discussing his failures, successes, prejudices, ambitions etc with his boss; it is another matter to expect him to do this with a stranger. There are serious questions of security;

subjects have no wish to have their job histories discussed outside their own immediate line of command. Usually the subject is at a lower level of management than the interviewer. It is not unlikely that some subjects will meet interviewers again in real life situations where the interviewer's knowledge can influence the subject's career. The knowledge that this could happen tends to influence the behaviour of the subject during the interview. He may wish to present a favourable image of himself to ensure he will be well regarded by the interviewer should he ever be considered for employment by him. He will be unwilling to discuss mistakes and failures, preferring successes, particularly those which illustrate his fitness for promotion or a change of job.

The third method was chosen because its advantages outweigh the disadvantages. There are the problems of artificiality and interpretation of the brief by the subject but these are outweighed by the freedom he feels in expressing his feelings and ideas. A subject is far more likely to allow anger or irritation to show, or to discuss failures and difficulties, if he can be seen to be discussing fictitious incidents. This does not prevent him from colouring his simulated behaviour with his own experiences and feelings as there can be no clear line between simulated and 'real' behaviour.

Having chosen this particular method, we discussed and agreed the general parameters of the job histories to be written in terms of age, seniority and general performance rating of the subject. We chose to write the histories around middle management jobs held by people who were in the age group 25–40 and who were putting up an adequate performance in their present job. They were capable of a satisfactory performance now in a job one level higher, but for which there were no immediate promotion prospects.

This is the part of any management population which is the most difficult to appraise constructively and motivate to maintain or improve performance. People whose performance constantly exceeds the requirements of the job will usually break out into a higher level job one way or another. Those who are not performing adequately may be dealt with in a number of ways ranging from careful counselling through threatening to sacking or demotion.

It is the adequate performers who have problems of continuing motivation. A man's manager often has little to offer either materially or in the promise of future promotion to such people, yet in his own interest, that of the subject and of the organization, he must try to raise and sustain job performance. In any case most staff, like most members of the population, will be average in their performance, whereas the organization often looks for better than average performance in a large share of its staff at all levels. It seeks to achieve this through appraisal, its monetary and status reward system and by the general techniques of motivation.

From these considerations a range of case studies was developed which could cover requirements for any mix of managers subjected to performance review interview training. The case of Victor (Victoria when appropriate) Ridsdale and his boss, Francis (Frances when appropriate) George Bean is typical of those developed for the course. Ridsdale, at 35, appears to have levelled off in his present job in spite of a promising start some years ago. He has developed the job since he came into it and is still of an innovative turn of mind, although recent ideas do not appear to have been appreciated by Bean. Ridsdale is frustrated by his present situation and can see little promise for the future. By no means a perfect performer himself, Bean has made a number of clumsy mistakes in his relationship with Ridsdale recently. Whilst bearing this in mind, he has to discover where Ridsdale can improve his performance and his attitude to his job, and motivate him accordingly. The Ridsdale story, as described in the brief issued to Bean (the interviewer) is one of a rather brash, petulant young man who is beginning to overstep his area of responsibility and who possibly needs constraining in this respect. This is quite different from the Ridsdale story as described in the brief issued to Ridsdale (the subject). One criterion for success in the interviews is to compare how much of the Ridsdale point of view is made evident to the interviewer. Ridsdale is Bean's direct subordinate yet some subjects are appraised by managers once (even twice) removed from them in the hierarchy. To accommodate interviewers who have to work in this way appropriate histories were also prepared.

Additional teaching aids

In planning the training we considered the use of various

additional aids to learning. The use of a 'demonstration' or 'model interview' was considered in planning the course. We ruled it out. Our main consideration in doing so arose from the high probability of the style demonstrated being taken as *the* way to conduct an appraisal interview. This was in direct conflict with the aims of the course, of which one was to develop not only skill but awareness in each manager of the need to vary his style according to situation.

Apart from this, if a 'model' interview were taken as a stereotype, interviews would fail as a result of individual subjects reacting to inappropriate treatments. Attempts by interviewers to imitate a demonstrator's style for one subject would be bound to go awry with other subjects, each reacting differently to the interviewer's approach. Generally interviews would fail early, with consequent loss of confidence by the interviewer and a loss of valuable learning experience for him and for the observers.

It is interesting to note that, as tutors' skills have improved, we find them illustrating a teaching point by demonstration. This seems to work well because at this stage in the course trainees have had experiences which demonstrate the need for flexibility of style and approach. In other words, the risk of a particular style being taken as a stereotype has been lessened at this juncture.

Early courses in the series were run without benefit of electronic aids although in our original planning we considered the use of audio and video tape recorders. At this stage we considered their use to be too distracting and in any case our tutors felt they lacked skill in using them. Later, as tutors' skills and confidence developed, we realized the benefit of more powerful tools in revealing shortcomings in interview performance. We therefore began to experiment with video and audio equipment. Now both are used and our experiences are described in the following chapter.

It is appropriate here to describe the effects of giving members an audio cassette recording of their two interviews. At first tutors only used the cassette as evidence to resolve differences occurring during the tutorial immediately after the interview and subsequently for research purposes.

It was quickly realized that if trainees could keep a record of their performance it would be of benefit. They could remind themselves again of recurring faults or how much they improved as a form of preparation before conducting future appraisal interviews.

The trainers were somewhat cynical of the use which the cassette might subsequently have. However, they have been constantly surprised to discover how often people have done what they hoped. Additionally, some managers have used their own tape as substitute or emergency training for other managers who had not attended the course. This use was not only a bonus but also indicative of the satisfaction people felt in the quality of their learning.

8
Managing and tutoring the course

The approach used on the course starts with the premise that no progress can be made in improving an interviewer's performance until illusion has been removed. Everyone presents an image to others which differs from the image he believes he is presenting. In the appraisal interview situation this is often starkly evident to the subject but not the interviewer. The reverse is also true: the subject's self-image differs from that perceived by the interviewer. This phenomenon acts as a barrier to communication, and causes a chain of misinterpretations and changes of course which serve greatly to reduce the interview's effectiveness. The trick is to convince the interviewer of this state of affairs. Once this has been done he should be able to take remedial action with the help of guidance from the tutors.

The basic purposes of practical work on the course are thus to:

1 Point out the difference between the interviewer's self-image and that perceived and interpreted by the subject.
2 Discuss and explain how it has come about in particular instances and the effect it has had on the course of an interview.
3 Enable individual interviewers to develop a strategy and practise the necessary skills to reduce 1 above to a minimum, and to increase the probability that the interview will change the subject's performance for the better.

Framework of the course

The purpose of the lectures and discussions is to outline the

63

techniques of effective interviewing and increase awareness of the psychological aspects of appraisal and motivation. All the theoretical and discussion sessions are based upon chapter 4 in part I. There is some formality in the approach but they are conducted as discussions, not lectures, with participants free to interpret and comment as they see fit. The theoretical work forms the basis of the ideas and skills used and applied in the practical sessions. For instance, interviewers learn about the adverse effect of leading questions or closed questions and practise asking more effective questions during the interviews. On the first day the emphasis is on improving the subject's capacity for work. Course members are encouraged to identify inadequacies in the subject's knowledge or skill as shown by his performance. They are directed to use the first practice sessions mainly to gain the subject's acceptance of these inadequacies and his commitment to improve, whilst not overlooking the value of acknowledging and building upon successes. On the second day they discuss motivation; they are given the opportunity of examining motivating factors in the practice interviews which follow and to bring about an increase in the subject's inclination to work.

Time is allocated as follows during practice interview sessions:

Interview (preferably without interruption)	30 mins
Completion of analysis forms by subject and interviewer	5 mins
Analysis by observers under tutorial guidance	10–15 mins
Critical comments by subject of interviewer	5–10 mins
	55 mins
Changeover, repeat cycle with new interviewer and subject	5 mins

Briefs for the first practice interviews are issued to interviewers about two weeks before the course, briefs for the second session are issued on the evening before they are used. Originally, for the first practice sessions, subjects were drawn from outside the course but difficulties over supplying subjects caused us to look at the possibility of using subjects from the course itself. This has the added advantage of interviewers experiencing the subject's point of view under training conditions.

This necessitates the use of two different job histories to avoid subjects and appraisers knowing both sides of the case. So in all, four different job histories are used on each course, two for the first day and two for the second.

The master tutor conducts the theoretical sessions and the assembly analysis following the practical sessions. One tutor to each syndicate of three course members manages the syndicates, ensuring the arrival at the correct time of subjects, and conducts tutorial sessions following (and occasionally during) interviews.

The role of the tutors

The managerial element of tutoring consists mainly of time management. All syndicates must have completed a cycle at the allotted time or the next cycle cannot be run. Because of this, one of the tutors is also course manager acting as a general progress chaser and ensuring that each tutor works to the scheduled time.

Using time to best effect in tutoring is always a difficulty. In a session where the interviewer has much progress to make, the tutor may feel that he needs far more time than he has been allocated. He is therefore tempted to try and cram a minute or two more into a particular teaching point. Even with a relatively skilled interviewer who has less to learn, the tutor is often faced with time problems because the interviewer and the observers frequently have opinions and ideas they wish to exchange and explore. Tutors approach the problem of time management with two important training concepts in mind. First, as a general rule people can only improve skill by short simple steps and progress must be immediately recognizable by the trainee. Secondly, if too many factors are dealt with at one time too much is attempted and failure and disillusion follow. Each tutor therefore concentrates on the one or two most significant factors requiring attention by the interviewer. He will seek to improve skill in these *one* or *two* factors so that after the next interview, the interviewer can recognize an improvement. For instance, a tutor may note that an interviewer:

(a) talks for 80 per cent of the time

(b) uses too many questions beginning 'Do you not think that....?' (This almost always becomes a leading question)

(c) abandons useful topics before he gets to the kernel of the problem

(d) fidgets uncertainly with his pencil

(e) interrupts the subject too often

(f) always defends the organization when the subject raises a critical point.

This set of faults is by no means uncommon and this is in fact a shorter list than usual. Many of these points will be noted by the observers and the tutor will have to ensure they are allowed to bring them up. He has to decide which *one* or *two* factors he needs to concentrate on and how best to deal with them. Generally he will go for the factor(s) which:

(a) have the most deleterious effect on the quality of the information the interviewer is getting

and if not inconsistent with (a)

(b) where the most significant improvement can be made next time the interviewer performs.

In the example above the tutor may concentrate on the interviewer's penchant for talking too much and for asking leading questions. Talking too much is common when trainees carry out their first interview on the course and takes care of itself. The discussion following the interview reveals, often to the surprise of the interviewer, how much information he has 'lost' because he talked too much. The impact of this revelation is such that interviewers usually talk less in their next interviews.

Leading questions are rather more difficult. They may be verbal mannerisms: 'do you not think that...?' frequently turns out to be a mannerism. This may present the tutor with some difficulty; by definition, mannerisms are difficult to eradicate. How does the tutor direct the energies of the syndicate towards the key factors he has decided need attention? First, he does *not* do it by assertion, by checking off the incidence of faults and then predicting the likely effects of these on the interview. Particularly in early interviews this leads to immediate defensiveness on the part of the interviewer: he will seek to show from evidence of the subject's behaviour that, if present, these faults had no deleterious effects. The observers may also jump to the interviewer's defence and the tutor then has a verbal battle on his hands. He will need to bring all his persuasiveness to bear, appealing to theory and to his own experience, or referring to 'cases' either real, imaginary, or composite, to back up his standpoint. If he is lucky he may eventually get compliance '. . . well if you say so I'll try it. . .'; if he is unlucky he may end up with an 'agree to differ' situation.

The strength of the approach used in the course is that subjects react 'naturally' to the interviewer's approach and are prepared to discuss their true feelings about the treatment they receive. The tutor therefore cannot prime the subject to react to a faulty style in order to bring out a particular lesson. Yet the subject is his strongest asset. The tutor can neither predict how the subject will react to the interview, nor can he be sure to have read accurately the outward signs made by the subject. So the tutor must tread warily in interpreting reactions and relating them to the interviewer's technique. The subject will have given verbal and behavioural signs of his reactions and the observers will have witnessed them. But the observers are often as unskilled as the interviewer and may not bring them out in their comments; the tutor must therefore seek to do so. Having heard the general comments made by both observers and called for clarification and amplification as necessary, the tutor must then draw on the observers' perceptions about the factors he is seeking to pursue. In pursuing the problem of leading questions, for example, he will refer to question technique specifically. The approach must be non-directive; he must not be seen to ask leading questions himself. So a sequence of questions by the tutor might be:

'What did you think of the questions he asked?'

'What effect did they have?'

'What information does the interviewer have now about . . . which he didn't have before the interview?'

'Was there anything you would have wished to find out which didn't come out?'

'Why did this information not come out?'

Somewhere here the observers, and possibly the interviewer, would conclude that the questions themselves had some bearing on why some of the information sought was not forthcoming. The interviewer can then lead on to 'What was it about the questions...' and so on until he is able to demonstrate that leading questions spoiled the interviewer's performance. Then, when the observers and interviewer are convinced, from recalling the interview the tutor can begin tutoring on leading questions, how they occur and why they are asked.

Why are leading questions asked? Sometimes they result from a verbal mannerism but usually the fault lies deeper. On exploring the topic, observers and interviewers conclude that the reason lies in the interviewer's desire to lead the subject to a particular solution, often before the problem itself has been exposed. So the interviewer is in the unenviable situation of having a solution available and of attempting to find a problem to which he may apply it. This follows from his belief that the scanty evidence in the brief enables him to know roughly what the subject's problem is. He feels concern for this and seeks to bring the subject to realize the 'problem' by asking questions to lead him there. Often this is not the problem at all and the subject hedges off this area; he sees no value in pursuing the topic and so the information gained is scanty.

Having worked on the key factors and promoted discussion in strategies to correct faults, the tutor brings the subject back into the syndicate to compare ratings on the interview analysis form and to get him to amplify these by reference to the interview. Again, the tutor seeks by open questions to produce evidence of the effect of the interviewer's approach on the subject's response.

A superficial reaction to this technique may be that the tutor behaves in a manner which he often criticizes interviewers for using: seeking by questioning to lead his 'subject' to a predetermined solution. But there is one important difference. The tutor is discussing behaviour which the interviewer has demonstrated and which observers and subject have seen. They may not all perceive these effects in the same way but all have seen them. The tutor is seeking to clarify what these effects have been and to discover and demonstrate what a particular behaviour pattern has cost the interviewer in quality and quantity of information and in the quality of the relationship he set up with the subject.

It will be seen that the tutor's role is to reveal rather than convince. In this situation he cannot afford to fail; for if his trainees do not 'see' they will not be convinced. He must therefore tread carefully, uncovering each point by reference to what people have seen and heard, not by reference to his experience, his opinion, his own preferred style of interviewing. Only when trainees, and particularly the interviewer, are convinced by what they have had revealed can he call upon these factors and upon theory, finally to back up his case.

Tutors' use of audio-visual equipment

The previous chapter has described how audio-visual equipment was considered, but not used until tutors were skilled or confident enough to tackle the hazards of handling cassette recorders and later closed-circuit TV. It is interesting to note that both are powerful media, but TV, approached with care, found easier acceptance from trainees.

Both media have to be used sparingly and only to assist in establishing the one or two most important development steps for the interviewer, to take next. Unless used in this way the media take over, are extremely time consuming and almost always direct attention away from the important learning points.

Fixed focus, wide angle lenses and black and white TV allowed the use of available light so successfully that the presence of the camera was totally forgotten within seconds of the start of practical work.

Audio cassette recordings to keep also make their contribution by providing a personal record of the interview and sometimes the main training points derived from it.

Observers

The role of the observers is to analyse the interview, to classify the various behaviour styles displayed and to relate these to the situational background of the interview. They are asked to comment on these points, and on the appropriateness of the interviewer's technique and on how he can improve. To help them in this task they are provided with the Appraisal Interview Observation Sheet (AIOS) and guidance notes on its use. This sheet is also used by tutors (see figures 3 and 4 on pages 71–72).

At first observers are diffident about making critical comment, presumably because they feel that they will be making similar mistakes themselves in their practice interviews. However, they soon overcome this and their contribution is most valuable. In many cases, quite naturally, interviewers are more willing to accept critical comment from those whom they regard as their peers than from the tutors, and an observer can usually be far more direct than the tutor.

Both observers and interviewers are assisted in judging the interviewer's success by a comparison of the declared objectives with those achieved. The Situation Analysis and Interview Plan (SAIP) described in the next chapter asks them to state their objectives and tutors ask each interviewer what his objectives are before the interview begins. The AIOS asks observers to comment under (c) on what the interaction achieved. This enables some comparison of achieved and declared objectives to be made. Probably the most significant 'skill' taught to managers in any form of interactive skills training is that of listening. For this purpose (a) of the AIOS is devoted to some estimate by observers and tutors of the time each interviewer devoted to listening to the subject. Most interviewers listen for only 25 per cent of the time and subjects for 75 per cent, when the balance in most cases ought to be the other way round. This section of the AIOS is useful in telling interviewers when they talk too much and in demonstrating the effect this has had on the interview.

Section (b) of the AIOS is to help observers and tutors to classify the interviewer's style, and to compare this with what was appropriate in terms of the situational background and the behaviour of the subject. By no means should an interviewer aim at only one style throughout. There may be times when an authoritarian style is required and when the interview needs to be very much a goal setting operation; for other parts of the interview a consultative style may be more appropriate, coupled with a problem solving approach. The tutor must show observers and interviewers that no absolute value can be attached to any one style or type of interview, only value in terms of how appropriate they were in the context of the situation as a whole. This encourages interviewers to exper-

Figure 3

APPRAISAL INTERVIEW OBSERVATION SHEET

Note the things the interviewer says or does which affect the interview.

What was said/what was done	What effect you think it had

ASSESSMENT

(a)   Time balance of interview   % appraiser   % appraisee   % nothing   ~~Listening~~

(b)   Style — AUTHORITARIAN   BENEVOLENT   CONSULTATIVE
        PARTICIPATIVE   *Int' Style . Was it appropriate*

(c)   What did the interaction achieve?   *Were dev's achieved*

Figure 4
GUIDANCE NOTES FOR AIOS

Please note positive and negative points during the appraisal interview using the form.

Points to consider
Opening
Was the opening:
   at-ease putting; anxiety raising; off putting; formal; casual; severe; obscure?

Middle
Is the appraiser:
   sensitive to subject's feelings?
   listening?
   using good/bad question techniques?
   following a purposeful path?
   making his objectives clear?
   varying the pace?

Is there:
   rapport?
   an inclination to agree?

Are the needs of the following being expressed:
   individual?
   managerial?
   organizational?

Is the appraiser's style appropriate?

Who is dominating the interview?

Ending
Was the subject left:
   high?
   low?
   sullen?
   content?
   motivated?
   crushed?
   rejecting the appraisal?

Was the appraisal:
   a step forwards?
   a step backwards?
   a non-event?

After the interview complete section 4 of the form.

iment. Some have never even suspected that alternative styles to their own exist. Often when interviewers are accused of being authoritarian at the wrong time they have confessed that they do not know of any other style.

Interviewer's feelings

There are other difficult points which need to be discussed and cleared up. One arises out of feelings of security. Managers' comments lead to the observation that they feel more secure behind the mask of authoritarianism or benevolence and within the 'listen-support' or 'tell-listen' type of interview. 'What', they ask, 'will my subordinates think of me if I ask them their opinion about a problem? They expect me to know the answer...' Remarks such as these indicate an underlying misconception about their role. They apparently feel that their subordinates expect more of them than is truly the case. They appear to think that they are expected to be omniscient and perhaps to know more about their subordinates' jobs than the subordinates themselves. This may be a reason why many managers are not as effective as they should be at appraisal interviewing. When this problem is raised the tutor needs to bring the discussion round to convincing the manager that, in asking for opinions and inviting participation from subordinates, he is displaying not weakness but strength. He is showing them that he recognizes their abilities and knowledge and is strong enough to use them and channel them.

Old habits die hard; the problem just described is a manager's bad habit when thinking about his job. There are also bad behavioural habits. The leading question has been mentioned before. It is of little value, and indicates to the subject what a 'desirable' answer will be. The habit of asking leading questions is a difficult one to break. How are you on tact? Do you feel that you get on with people? Did you enjoy the responsibility...? I suppose you delegated...? will tell the interviewer nothing of value about the subject, yet during the second set of practice interviews a number of such questions are still being asked and pointed out by tutors and observers. Most observers do pick them out so this leads to the belief that they will be watched for in the future when observers are interviewing. The Interview Analysis Form (IAF) (see figure 5

73

opposite) is a simple instrument for comparing the interviewer's self image with the image he presents to the subject.

Its intention is to induce both parties to commit themselves to an opinion about the behaviour of the interviewer and then to use differences thus highlighted as the medium for discussion about how these differences came about. The number scores given in the IAF are of course not meant to be absolute and, with such a small sample, can never be used to prove anything; they can be used to illustrate attitudes, points of view and typical behaviour. From experience we know that a difference in score of two or more is needed to provide worthwhile points of discussion. Of course it is sometimes useful to note that both parties have similar perceptions of the interviewer so like scores can also be useful. But differences usually provide more worthwhile discussion on why they exist, how they came about and the inferences for the interview. The IAF does not seek to ascribe high values to one or other of any of the opposites in the matrix in section 2 of the form. Each of these 'postures' (of eg 'rigidity' or 'flexibility') must be seen in the whole context of the interview. The first edition of the IAF had all the factors to which people attach low value at the 1 end of the matrix and all the high value factors at the 6 end. In the assembly analysis, when all the data generated by the IAF was presented to the course members, they tended to add the scores given by subjects and to compare these totals with others' scores. An interviewer who had a higher numerical sum than another thus regarded himself as the better interviewer. No amount of persuasion by tutors on the fallacy in such an assumption appeared to have any great effect on this; the matrix was therefore 'scrambled' so that such summation was no longer possible. It served to bring attention back to the IAF as an instrument for comparison rather than measurement. A typical assembly analysis is shown and analysed on page 79.

Rule no 1 for any appraisal interview must be 'don't project'. In other words do not try to impose your values on the subject, do not attempt to judge his performance and attitude to his job in terms of your own feelings about things as they are not comparable in this way. The considerate-inconsiderate and indifferent-concerned axes in section 2 of the IAF are often useful in demonstrating to interviewers that they are projecting too much. When a subject scores the interviewer as 'inconsiderate' and 'indifferent to common problems', the subsequent

74

Figure 5
INTERVIEW ANALYSIS FORM

Appraiser   Name:

Subject   Name:

1 **BOTH PARTICIPANTS**
How satisfied were you with the other person's response to you during the appraisal?
    Appraiser's mark   X
    Subject's mark   O

Very |___|___|___|___|___| Very
dissatisfied   1   2   3   4   5   6   satisfied

2 **BOTH PARTICIPANTS**
What number best describes the *appraiser's* behaviour?
Mark each line.

(a)   Rigid |___|___|___|___|___| Flexible
                     1   2   3   4   5   6

(b)   Frank |___|___|___|___|___| Reticent
                     1   2   3   4   5   6

(c)   Considerate |___|___|___|___|___| Inconsiderate
                     1   2   3   4   5   6

(d) Indifferent to |___|___|___|___|___| Concerned about
   common problems   1   2   3   4   5   6   common problems

3 **APPRAISERS ONLY**
How satisfied were you with your performance during the

Very |___|___|___|___|___| Very
dissatisfied   1   2   3   4   5   6   satisfied

4 **APPRAISERS ONLY**
How nearly did you achieve your objective?

Completely |___|___|___|___|___| Not at all
               1   2   3   4   5   6

BOTH PARTICIPANTS
List future *actions* agreed by (a) appraiser (b) subject

(a)   (b)

analysis often reveals that the interviewer has been talking too much anyway and has been projecting strongly. Subjects and interviewers drawn from an appraisal course consisting of sales managers often have problems of projection. Subjects express strong feelings about being pushed by the interviewer; interviewers accuse subjects of brashness, observers record the interview as 80 per cent interviewer talking, authoritarian and 'tell-sell'. The conclusion to be drawn from this is that it probably results from a salesman's training and mode of operation. He is trained to project, to overcome objections and to press home his point of view. Such behaviour is entirely inappropriate in appraisal interviewing. Usually no trouble is experienced in weaning interviewers away from the projection problem once they have its effects demonstrated and discussed. Like the phenomenon of the one style approach and that of not listening enough, once interviewers are aware of the existence and of the value of alternatives they are only too ready to pursue them and gain experience in their use.

Questions 4 and 5 of the form were introduced as a result of experience on early courses. Tutors reported difficulty in inducing interviewers to bear in mind the performance improvement element of appraisal review. In working at building rapport, obtaining information and seeking motivators in the subject's make-up, interviewers were neglecting to agree or impose objectives and actions for the future. Early versions of the form left this section as 'any supporting comments?'—a question which was far too loosely directed.

Question 4 asks the interviewer to declare how well he feels he met the objectives he set and which he declared to the tutor at the start of the interview. This question has to be treated flexibly by the tutor since an interviewer will be prepared to change his objectives as the information he obtains modifies his original view. Question 5, answered by both participants compares their view of the actions agreed by both. It first points the interviewer toward the need for specific *actions* rather than *intentions* as a prime output from the interaction. Secondly, as it usually shows wide differences in view, it emphasizes the need for precision and for care in the choice of language when agreeing or laying down what actions are expected.

The point about intentions and actions is that a general intention like '...has agreed to show more tact in future', is often an indication of information being obtained only at a superficial level. Further probing may enable the interviewer to write, for instance, '...when requesting help from the technical department will find out priorities for their work load before assessing the relative priority of the job he had requested'. Here an intention has been translated into an action plan with a far better chance of success. 'We shall meet more frequently...' is imprecise; 'I will arrange to meet him once each month to assess progress and discuss difficulties...' is a precise statement of future action.

The assembly analysis

The assembly analysis is used to share the experiences of course members and tutors. There is a persistent tendency (see page 79) for subjects to judge an interviewer's effectiveness in terms of what he gives away materially rather than in terms of quality of relationship, reinforcement and motivation. Any worthwhile comments by subjects are recorded on the IAF; they are discussed first in syndicates and then in the assembly analysis.

Discussion during the assembly analysis is centred on differences of two or more in sections 1 and 2 of the IAF as in syndicate meetings. The tutor draws out the main points thus demonstrated and, by referring to theory expounded earlier, is able to reinforce the lessons learned. There is rarely any reluctance on the part of interviewers to discuss their mistakes although defensiveness is often encountered at this stage. It is here once again that the problems of artificiality and of 'insufficient information' are raised, frequently as a smoke screen to hide inadequacies and often deep seated prejudices about the role of management. Although by no means every objector allows himself to be openly convinced, most are influenced by pressure from their more open minded colleagues: this is shown by their improved performance in the second set of interviews.

As stated at the beginning of this section, stripping away illusion is the basis of progress in this area of training. The assembly analysis is a review session in which progress can be checked by tutors, and in which it can be reinforced by reference to the total experiences of the group and to the theory already discussed. It is an important if not vital part of the course.

Assembly analysis takes place once paper work has been completed at the end of each session of practice interviews.

The following is attempted by the discussions:

1 To release and share the emotion that invariably occurs amongst people attempting to change or acquire a skill.
2 To drive home the teaching points of the theory sessions.
3 To drive home the lessons learned through the tutors in the practice sessions.
4 To lay the foundations for future self-assessment and personal feedback after the real interviews that will take place on the job.
5 To build self-confidence in the personal level of skill that the manager has displayed, so that he feels at least adequate to cope with the task of performance review interviewing.

Groups differ in their reactions to the training, so the emphasis placed on each objective will vary from course to course. However, all the objectives are attempted with each group; in the event some discussions under each heading will take place with each group.

The data from the IAF will have been displayed under the name of each interviewer. An example of an actual analysis is shown in figure 6 opposite. Before the 'unveiling' members of the group are asked to bring up any general comments on their experiences during the practice interviews. This gives the first indication of any general emotional reactions to the practical sessions. After these have been discussed each member of the group is given the opportunity to highlight the main events of his interview; to explain the discrepancies in the scores circled; to say what he achieved by the interview, what he had learned from it, and what he would do differently next time. The observers and tutors are encouraged to join in and make their own views heard about each interview.

The use of the assembled data illustrated in figure 6, can be demonstrated by a comparison of two practice interviews. There is clearly a difference between interviewer B and interviewer C, even though they interviewed the same subject AFW. B's self-assessments, shown in the left hand column, are mar-

Figure 6

ASSEMBLY ANALYSIS

	A	B	C	D	E	F	G	H	J
Satisfaction with other's response	5-6	(6-3)	5-6	4-4	5-5	(4-6)	6-5	(5-2)	5-6
Rigid (1) Flexible (7)	4-5	(5-3)	5-6	3-3	(3-5)	5-5	6-6	(4-1)	5-6
Frank (1) Reticent (7)	3-4	(5-2)	6-5	5-4	(4-2)	3-2	6-6	(2-5)	(5-3)
Considerate (1) Inconsiderate (7)	4-4	(3-5)	4-3	5-4	3-2	(5-2)	6-3	(2-6)	(5-1)
Indifferent (1) Concerned (7)	(5-3)	(5-2)	5-5	4-5	5-6	(4-6)	6-4	(5-2)	5-6
Satisfaction with own performance	4	2	5	3	3	3	5	3	3
Achievement of objectives	4	6	2	6	4	3	2	6	5
Time balance	60/40	70/30	50/50	60/40	50/50	40/60	50/50	80/20	40/60

AFW (under A, B) · PH (under E) · PDW (under H)

A-J are interviewers. AFW, PH, PDW are subjects. Interviewers' ratings in left hand column. Subjects' ratings in right hand column. Differences > 2 are circled.

79

kedly different from those given by his subject in the right hand column, whereas C's ratings are nearly coincident with his subject's. Why is this? Both interviewers are asked to account for their pattern of ratings.

B may admit that he talked too much; that he did not listen or that his strategy was wholly inappropriate for that subject. He may account for the difference of 3 on the 'frank/reticent' scale by saying that he saw himself as guarded and reticent and that the subject saw him as more frank; however, he was seen as 'inconsiderate' but thought himself to be 'considerate'. It could be that being what he thought to be considerate is actually seen as being frank and somewhat uncaring! A self-rating of 2 (out of 6) on 'satisfaction with own performance' clearly indicates that the interviewer realized that the interview did not go very well; he may need some 'supportive' comments to help him maintain his confidence. A shared analysis of this kind could help him understand better his interviewing style and its impact on his staff.

When it comes to his turn, C may appear smug about the apparent concordance between his self-ratings and his subject's. His 5 on 'satisfaction with own performance' and his 2 on 'achievement of objectives' also signal some complacency. If this is so the observer only has to comment that the interview was cosy and achieved little, for example, in order to focus discussion on to the need for the manager to be more purposeful and set more appropriate objectives. Appraisal interviewing cannot be taught, it can only be learned. The assembly analysis discussion, through the signalling device of the pairs of ratings should crystallize and enhance the learning experiences provided by the practical exercises.

The assembly analysis on the first day is directed at the question 'did the interviewer achieve a development step with the subject?' That is, did the interview result in the identification of a piece of knowledge, an aspect of skill or change of behaviour that the subject could acquire which would make him better at his job? If so, was a realistic plan agreed to take this development step and were both the participants committed to the plan?

After the second set of practice interviews the discussion is enlarged to include the question: 'did the subject experience motivation growth as the result of the interview?' That is, were any psychological blocks removed, brakes released or accelerating forces applied, which would lead to the subject working harder and enjoying his job more?

The final assembly analysis ends with a discussion reinforcing the need for the course participants to act as their own 'feedback and monitoring device' after all their future performance review interviews.

Summary

The key issues within the training methods adopted can be summarized under four headings: unfreezing and unlearning; concept formation; tutored practical work; self analysis and self development.

1 UNFREEZING AND UNLEARNING

For a skill to be acquired the learner must first value and then start to develop it. Illusions about the managerial process and delusions about personal competence have to be stripped away. So, invariably, any workshop or seminar on staff development should start with a general discussion of the whole process, so that misconceptions and anxieties are exposed and the managers prepared for the new concepts and the behaviour they imply. Various exercises and visual aids, such as optical illusion slides, are useful at this stage.

It is interesting to note that the need, and therefore the time allocation, for this component of the training has decreased over the 14 years' experience with this workshop.

2 CONCEPT FORMATION

The definition of staff appraisal developed at Bradford is put across as follows at the beginning of training.

> Staff development aims to increase the performance of a person in their *existing* job, and so to increase their satisfaction with *that job*. A secondary objective, once the above has been achieved, is to agree the plans for the individual's next job and to make preparations for that job through additional experiences and training.
>
> Staff development is not specifically concerned with assessing, evaluating or establishing quantitative standards con-

cerning a person's current job performance. However, such assessments could be discussed if they were judged by the manager to be relevant to the task of *adding to* the ability and motivation of the member of staff for the current job. Similarly, objectives and target setting could be used as a part of the process as long as they result in the individual learning and becoming committed to a change in behaviour that leads to *increased job performance* and the organization learning through the manager. This requires joint commitment to an action plan that leads to more satisfaction or motivation within the employee. It is important to note that it is not necessary to go through an evaluation stage when trying to get staff to change their behaviour. Also staff development requires considerable skill, and therefore training, to accomplish: that is why you are here.

It is certainly not easy to wean managers of their inclination, perhaps deeply conditioned by their own experiences and professional training, to assess past work performance by attaching some differential economic value to work achieved. Extrapolating a measure of current achievement to future attainments is attractive to managers. Perhaps such acts of judgement of worth and potential provide feelings of power. However, if they distract, as they invariably do, from the task of adding to the capacity and motivation to perform the current job, then they undermine the chances of gaining immediate increments of performance. It is of the utmost importance that this key concept of staff development is backed up by *separate* organizational practices in the field of merit rating and assessing managerial potential.

Once this key concept has been inculcated then it is relatively straightforward to get across the technique of identifying, through the skilled use of questions and statements, what the individual needs to do *next* in his job, what the manager needs to do *next* for the individual and then to devise mutually committing action plans for the agreed events. The danger here is to make it sound all too easy, but the next step in the process usually cures that idea.

One of the great problems in the behavioural sciences is the gap between a concept and its application. In training for engineering this skills gap has been recognized by the weeks spent on practical training at all levels. But many managers still resist this need for practical work in management training, thinking that to understand a concept is enough for a clever person to apply it. Unfortunately many training courses in the behavioural field use practical exercises to teach a concept. Such 'experiential learning' is a powerful way to get an idea across, but can do the subject a disservice by leaving managers with the belief that they acquired the skill of application along with the understanding.

Giving 'feedback' to senior managers about the effects and effectiveness of their interactions with a subordinate is no easy task. The selection, maintenance and development of teams of tutors has been a signficant factor in the growth of this approach to staff appraisal. The analysis of tutoring skills and the training of tutors has run in parallel with the work described here, and forms the subject of a separate IPM booklet (Taylor D S. *Performance Reviews*). Tutoring is itself a powerful learning experience for trainers and young managers. One organization recognized this point and took a 'cascade' approach to the process. They started the two-day workshops at the top of the organization, using 'outside' tutors. Then at each 'level' of management they identified those amongst the trainees who displayed tutorial skills and trained them further. They then used this group as the team of tutors to the next level of management. They claim that not only did this deepen the training within these managers but also gave extra insight into their management potential.

It is illuminating that there have been so few disasters arising from this high-risk form of training. Many managers have been severely shaken by the experience; a few have rejected it; but the great majority have reported that they gained a great deal from the experience of getting feedback through skilled handling of their learning by their tutors.

No skill of any consequence can be acquired, or significantly enhanced, as a result of just two days training. It is remarkable that so much does appear to be inculcated by the workshop described here. As this approach to staff development gained greater standing, experience, and confidence the emphasis within the training changed. It moved from a direct attempt to add to manager's skills towards laying the foundations for the skill to grow. This change of emphasis was reflected not only in the content of the 'teaching' component of the workshop, but also in the way in which the tutors handled the analysis and feedback within the syndicate groups. More effort was given to encouraging analysis of the 'performances' given by the syndicate members. The visual and audio aids were used less, giving more time for discussion within the groups and explanation from the tutors. On the second day the interviewers were expected to give a more thorough analysis of their own performance, and to work out for themselves how they could do it better. All these changes, some quite subtle, moved the workshop more towards training in self-coaching. However, if the tutor thought the participant was not responding, then the original approach of working on *exactly* what the interviewer did 'least well' and *exactly*, in strict behavioural and obtainable terms, what the interviewer should be attempting differently was used. If the managers could be given the technique and the willingness to do it for themselves, then this is regarded as the peak of tutorial attainment with the expectation that the skill would appear and develop during all the managerial experiences to come.

9
Overcoming role-play problems

It was necessary to provide material which could be readily manipulated by any manager from a variety of disciplines on any particular course. As all managers know (or feel familiar with) the elements of administration, we wrote job histories around the administrative details of the jobs described. The technical detail of these jobs was made deliberately sketchy and vague. This approach was chosen because:

1 It would be administratively difficult to provide practical material and subjects for each manager to discuss a job performance within his own particular discipline.
2 During practice interviews, observers drawn from the course are in attendance. They also learn by observation and later inform the interviewer of the impact of his style and technique. It is necessary for the observers too to have a common 'language' with the interviewer.
3 In any case, appraising the technical aspects of job performance is usually relatively easy. The real skill comes in analysing such factors as the subject's judgement and balance, his relations with others, his interaction with the organization, his decision making processes and the human effects of his decisions.

The early design of the course called for the use of subjects who were not members of the course. The provision of eight subjects for each of many courses in an organization which had locations spread across the UK caused distinct administrative difficulties. A first step towards reducing the need was made by using subjects from outside only on the first day, and on the second day providing the resource from course membership.

This also eased the pre-course preparation in that joining instructions were identical.

The final step was to dispense with outside subjects altogether. Members are now issued with two sets of briefs about a week before the course starts, half with those for Interviewer (A) and Subject (B), the remainder with Subject A and Interviewer B. Further briefs for Interviewer C and Subject D together with Subject C and Interviewer D are issued at the end of the first day for study overnight.

The use of role-play exercises causes problems for both interviewers and subjects alike.

INSUFFICIENT INFORMATION

The sketchy outlines supplied to interviewers cause them real problems of adjustment. Managers are accustomed to collecting information when faced with any problem. Where insufficient information is readily available they will arrange to uncover the less obvious. So their first reaction is to point out that there is not enough information about the subject's personality, or his duties, or some specific incident mentioned in the brief. It is therefore important that the tutor should lead them away from this approach and into the one they have now been trained in, namely to seek information from the subject. They are led back to the brief and asked to consider, from what they read there, how the subject is likely to react to the various issues they would wish to discuss and asked to plan to raise particular issues themselves in the way which would provoke the most useful response.

They also consider the various modes of behaviour they are likely to encounter on particular issues and plan a strategy to cope with them. In considering their approach to an interview, some managers see the subject as someone requiring strong corrective action or punishment because of things they read in (or read into) the brief. The tutor must point out that while this could be true, and could possibly be appropriate in a real life case, it would not be likely to give the interviewer much training in appraisal interviewing. The tutor then needs to change the proposed strategy to one of analysing the causes of the apparent behaviour of the subject, and indeed to discover if this behaviour is all that it appears to be. When discussing a point causing irritation to some parts of the organization described in a practice case, managers have been surprised to find that the subject's view of what he was doing was quite different, was well intentioned and believed by him to be well received by the organization. This does not seek to prove anything, it merely serves to illustrate the differences in perception which occur between people all the time.

DISCOMFORTS OF INTERVIEWERS

The interviewer's side of the cases used outlines a manager who, being human and working in a human organization, is less than perfect; he has himself made mistakes which have had an effect on the performance of the subject and on his relationship with him. This is the most frequent cause for complaint by managers preparing for their practice interviews. They ask how they can be expected to judge a subordinate's behaviour at work, to discuss his failures and successes with him, above all, how they can discuss their relationship with him when some of the problems described will have been made worse by the forgetfulness, rudeness and lack of consideration shown by the manager in the case. The tutor must point out that being human they will sometimes be in the wrong and the practice they get will stand them in good stead whenever they have to appraise someone under these conditions. The problem then often becomes one of preventing the interviewer from being too abject and apologetic, and of pointing out the impact this would have on the relationship in the future. Interviewers are also told that, in order to give them practice in operating in an imperfect world, the background information on the job histories also describes an imperfect company with an imperfect organization, and with all the consequent strains and problems between people and between departments.

The adjustment problems described are usually expressions of discomfort on the part of the managers. Not having enough information or being placed in what they see as a defensive position causes them to react in a way intended to gain more comfort. They wish to judge success in terms of a successful interview rather than in terms of a successful learning experience. They also complain about the general artificiality of the situation. They have not met the subject before whereas a manager usually sees his subordinate frequently. 'No manager worth his salt would allow a situation to go this far before correcting it', is a typical expression of this feeling.

It is interesting to note that few managers have complained about the artificial situation of having people watching and commenting on their interviews. This does have an effect, which they are prepared to discuss, but they rarely complain. In short, the tutor's job is to prepare the interviewers to achieve a state of mind where they are ready to accept the discomfort and even to see advantages in the very situation they have complained about. For example, the fact that the interviewer has not met the subject before can be seen as a powerful incentive to concentrate hard on building an effective relationship during the interview. It can also be seen as useful practice in ascertaining a subject's frame of mind by interpreting his gestures and reactions to the interviewer at first meeting.

In spite of careful handling of this discomfort problem by tutors, about half of the first practice interviews are less effective as training instruments than they might be; this is the result of inhibition on the part of interviewers and their tendency to fight the situation. In the second set of interviews this phenomenon disappears almost entirely. In spite of overt resistance by a very few managers, most overcome their doubts, accept the parameters of the exercise and approach their interview in a receptive state of mind.

Subjects are briefed to react as closely as possible to real life to the way they are treated by the interviewer. They are asked to note feelings which they would normally suppress, and to be prepared to discuss these and how they arose in the analysis session which follows each interview. For instance, an interviewer might say '. . . anyway I'm sorry we weren't able to adopt your plan but you might like to know that I have been able to use a lot of the ideas in. . .' The subject's reaction could easily be '. . . the old devil, he didn't think enough of the plan to put it through but he pinched a lot of the ideas that went into it—cheek!. . .' But he might feel it prudent to say '. . . I'm sorry too, that plan took a lot of time to prepare. . .' He would note the thoughts behind this rather bland statement and the remark which had brought the thoughts on and be prepared to discuss them later.

Much must be left to the imagination of the subject; it is difficult to advise him when he would be going beyond the bounds of the exercise. The advice given is to point out that anything they invent must not change the basic outline of the job history or give the interviewer a way out which avoids practising good interviewing. For instance, one interviewer's brief includes the point that the subject is not prepared to move to a distant unit in the company to gain a more responsible and more highly paid job. It would not be appropriate for the subject to intimate that he has now changed his mind and is prepared to move. The subject must keep in mind the objective of giving interviewers practice in appraising adequate performers for whom no immediate promotion prospects are available. If he does not allow the interviewer to find a way out of the impasse, the interviewer may find himself exploring the subject's motivation, why he does not want to move, what he can do to improve his performance (and hence possibly his potential for promotion) in his present job. He may also gain in experience in explaining to the subject that his future is constrained by his refusal to move, and outlining the various courses open to him.

In the analysis session after an interview, the subject's participation is vital. He can tell the interviewer how he reacted to his approach and his feelings about particular remarks or apparent implications. Since it is the quality of the interaction between interviewer and subject which is being judged, the subject should base his comments only on the quality of the relationship and on the act of communication between them.

Unfortunately some subjects have a tendency to cloud the issue by ascribing a positive value to factors outside this. The interviewer who has promised a company car, or rapid promotion, is often judged as an effective interviewer by the subject. Some subjects demonstrate a flaw in their thinking about their success or otherwise in gaining acceptance of ideas. Where their role indicates they have failed to get an apparently sound idea accepted, they explain this failure by saying the organization is at fault. If only the boss would make people do something, or the organization could be rearranged so that it could be compelled to accept the idea, the problem would be solved. Interviewers who accept or better still suggest such an authoritarian approach tend to be rated highly by such subjects. It requires careful and patient handling by tutors first of all to brief subjects not to judge by these criteria, and then to deal with the situation when some of them persist in doing so. It is sometimes necessary to wait until the subject has left the tutorial group; it can then be pointed out how unrealistic it would be for interviewers to accept values ascribed to what they have been able to give away in an imaginary situation. The tutor also has to point out again the value of practising appraisal interviewing where there is little to give away.

PREPARING FOR THE INTERVIEW

Some of the discomforts and difficulties mentioned above were alleviated in two ways.

The situation analysis and interview plan (SAIP see figure 7 opposite) was introduced to help overcome weaknesses in the interviewer's approach to the interview since it was found that they were often inadequately prepared.

Not only did interviewers have difficulty in remembering the outlines of the case they had read, but they were also inadequately prepared for the range of responses they received from the subjects. Interviewers were running out of steam after a few minutes and were often completely nonplussed by some retort from the subject. The SAIP enables the interviewer to examine each critical incident mentioned in the brief in terms of its likely effect on the organization and on the subject's behaviour during the interview. The interviewer is then led into formulating and stating his objectives and outlining a plan for the interview. This approach has proved most useful in encouraging interviewers to be thorough in their preparation. It has also enabled them to think out a particular way of asking a question so as to get the best and most informative response. People who have used the SAIP thoroughly have usually asked fewer leading questions and have handled the relationship far more smoothly and purposefully than those whose preparation has not been quite so painstaking.

The second method of preparation involves group briefing. An example of this occurs on the second day when group 1 has the interviewer's brief for Charles Thompson, Financial Controller, and the subject's brief for the Sales Supervisor, Ed Brown.

Group 2 will have corresponding briefs for the Chief Accountant, Peter Small and the Sales Manager, Al Phillips.

This grouping into two distinct 'sets' of participants enables

Figure 7

SITUATION ANALYSIS			YOUR INTERVIEW PLAN

APPRAISAL INTERVIEW—SITUATION ANALYSIS AND INTERVIEW PLAN

YOUR NAME............ APPRAISER............ SUBJECT..........

SITUATION ANALYSIS			YOUR INTERVIEW PLAN
Incident	Likely effect on individual and on organization	Resulting likely influence on subject's behaviour in interview	(Include remarks prepared for a specific purpose eg provoking, probing, summarizing, etc)
			OPENING (What style?)
			MIDDLE (Predict likely hangups)
SUMMARY OF YOUR OBJECTIVES FOR THE INTERVIEW APPRAISERS — A general objective is to aim for commitment, bearing these questions in mind: 1 How is he doing? 2 What are his problems? 3 What are his inclinations? 4 Where is he going?			**END** (How?) REMEMBER—KEEP YOUR APPROACH CONSTRUCTIVE

tutors to lay the groundwork for skills improvement and to alleviate some of the difficulties of discomfort already mentioned. Appendix A on page 113, shows that 45 minutes are allocated to preparation for the second practice interview sessions. During these sessions group I is segregated from group II and a tutor attached to each group. Before this segregation occurs both groups are asked to spend:

(i) about 15 minutes in considering ways in which an *appraiser*, Charles Thompson (I) and Al Phillips (II), can deal with the issues raised in his brief and how he will deal with the various responses possible on the part of their subjects, Peter Small (II) and Ed Brown (I).

(ii) the remaining time of approximately 30 minutes in considering, in their role of *subjects*, how they can give the most valuable learning experience to interviewers.

Assignment (I) is designed to assist in the process of familiarizing interviewers with the brief and in beginning the process of acquiring skill and flexibility. Assignment (II) is intended to overcome the 'wooden' response often encountered in role-playing situations, and again to assist in familiarizing members with the brief.

The tutor plays a non-directive role during this session, beginning by indicating that the group should discuss its assignment and can call on the tutor for comment as necessary. Often the group of six revert to reading their briefs. The tutor would then point out that it would be more profitable to talk rather than read. A further reminder about talking not reading may be needed but usually someone begins to talk at this juncture. One or more of the group might begin to describe how he sees the interviewer's situation and how he thinks he should deal with it. Talk ranges over the sort of person the subject seems to be, from the information in the interviewer's brief. This leads to discussion on how he should therefore be treated and the ways in which he can be expected to respond. When this process is well under way (usually after about five minutes) the tutor can begin to play his role. He does this by responding as the subject could to the approaches being discussed. He can, for instance, make the sort of response given by a subject who, because he needs to keep his job, shows compliance rather than commitment. He would demonstrate the sort of response a person in such a frame of mind might make.

For instance, in case study 2 involving Thompson, Financial Controller and Small, Chief Accountant, a critical incident is described in Thompson's brief where Small's attempt at installing a training scheme for training supervisors has apparently been thrown out by works management. The interaction would go something like this, with a discussion starting on the lines:

Member A — If Small had put his idea on works training instead of working on his own with the works manager, maybe his scheme would have come off instead of being thrown out.

Member B — So we tell him to try again and in future to put things like that through Thompson.

A — Yes, that would also cover some of the feelings he is bound to bring up about lack of contact with Thompson.

The discussion would go on in this vein, and to some effect but, judging the time to be right, the tutor would inject the sort of response such an approach *could* draw from Small himself:

Tutor — Im very sorry Mr Thompson, but I can't see how that helps me with my problem.

C (to tutor but seeking support from group) — But surely Thompson has a right to expect Small to put his ideas through him.

Tutor — Look Mr Thompson, I tried by best with this training scheme, worked evenings, discussed things with the production manager, thought everything was going well then . . .

A (catching on) — But look Peter, it didn't work did it; why?

Tutor — I don't know, the works manager just said the man didn't like me sticking my oar in, but . . .

A—Well, there you are, you should have come to me.

Tutor—Yes but how can I do that with problems like this. With respect Mr Thompson, I want to be my own man, and besides . . .

A—No it's obvious you need my support. Look, later on you tell me about the scheme and I'll get it through. Don't you think that's best Peter?

Turning to the rest of the group the tutor would point out that this is one response they *could* get. But what if instead they got:

Tutor—No, sorry, that just won't do. Now what we should do, Mr Thompson, is lay down a system by which all works people should receive this training. Please, would you issue a directive to that effect? Then the works manager will have to listen to me. After all, I'm sure you agree, the scheme is needed, and it's a good one. It's just that they are being so difficult.

And further interviewing practice would arise out of this simulated response from Peter Small.

During assignment (II) on these lines, the tutor is able to develop various responses within subjects by demonstrating various types of behaviour they might encounter from an interviewer. For instance, case study 3 involves Sales Supervisor, Ed Brown and his Manager, Al Phillips. The previous day Ed Brown, with an exciting idea in mind, has requested analysis of a competitor's product from the Technical Manager. When Brown leaves the Technical Manager he has the impression that, in spite of some concern about the laboratory's work load, the analysis will be forthcoming. But Phillips has other information in his brief and course members will often use this in typical fashion:

—Now look here Ed, you've been and upset the Technical Manager and there's hell to pay. I've had my boss on my back over it, and I'm not having that—now I want to know what you've been up to—and it had better be good!

From the first stuttering, astounded response he draws from subjects to this attack, the tutor can provoke the group members to actual frustration and anger where they begin to demonstrate how a man might actually respond in such a situation. Having demonstrated this he will then move on to a different approach, such as:

> —You told me you had a sample tested yesterday Ed. Was that when you saw the Technical Manager?

Group member — Yes

> —What happened? . . . and so on.

This briefing technique has been found to be valuable in delivering subjects to the practice sessions who are well briefed in the case outlines, and well prepared for the varying response a particular interviewing style can bring about. It pays off in the quality and depth of learning experiences it provides.

10

Surveying the results

Various studies have been completed, and more are under way, attempting to assess and evaluate the effectiveness of this 'skills' approach to adding to individual and organizational performance.

Such studies are notoriously difficult to design and then to generate data of sufficient quality to enable causal conclusions to be drawn. There is the further complication of 'bias of auspices', when the promulgators of the concepts and training produce evidence of its effectiveness themselves. Obtaining 'independent' evaluation data is methodologically more respectable but difficult to achieve in practice. The studies reported below are a mix of 'dependent' and 'independent' investigations, and are set out under the usual headings for the evaluation of training.

Reactions

The first 2,000 managers who attended the workshop were asked to complete a post-course questionnaire, and almost all those who replied reported that they had obtained a 'useful experience' that could be applied with benefit to their managerial tasks. Although reactions data is scientifically suspect it can have considerable 'social significance'. If chief executives, or previously sceptical influential managers, can be heard to say such skills training 'works' and authorize further investment of money and staff time in it, then this is taken within organizations (but not necessarily within the scientific community) as 'hard' evidence for the effectiveness of the procedures. To line managers such 'evidence' is regarded as far more 'significant' than any statistical tests. Of 12 manufacturing companies who made a start with this skills approach to staff development 10 have carried it through in depth in their organizations.

Learning

The organization that initiated the approach (Fisons plc) was also the first to carry out follow-up studies of the learning of the managers. Two interview/questionnaire, self-report studies were undertaken (first of 112 managers and then a more detailed study of 30 R and D managers) which attempted to assess the type and amount of learning that had taken place as a result of the course. These two studies indicated that the workshop had brought about increased awareness of the importance, and what could be done to improve, the processes of motivation; communication; information; and achievement of objectives and planning within the performance reviews they conducted with their staff.

A post-graduate student at Aston University carried out an independent study of the effects of the workshop in GKN-Sankey. He interviewed eight directors and 16 senior managers and reported that the major effects of the workshop were increasing the awareness of other people's jobs and problems and the need for closer communications. He also found that interpersonal relationships and more effective working relationships had developed as a result of the principles of the workshop being applied. A free-interview study of eight directors/senior managers of the Evode Group by two officials of the Rubber and Plastics Industry Training Board concluded that the workshop had resulted in improvements in the managers' skills of listening, interpreting, planning, questioning, reflecting, and reacting. In a further account of the Evode Scheme, it was reported that even highly resistant and sceptical managers had learned a great deal about themselves, as well as the skill of staff development, from the workshop.

An important point needs to be made about the process of evaluating training through questioning participants directly. It is that even though self-report data concerning the subsequent gains achieved from a training course is of doubtful value for validation purposes, the act of completing questionnaires for course evaluation purposes can give an additional learning experience for managers and provide a reminder of things learned on the course. The normative data that such techniques generate can then be fed back to the individuals to become a further spur to the acquisition of the skill.

Job behaviour

As the whole point of staff development skill is concerned with changing the behaviour of individuals, managers and organizations, attempts at measuring changes in behaviour should form the basis of any evaluation.

The two self-report studies carried out in Fisons, described above, provided the basis of a large scale questionnaire study of managers in one of the divisions of the company having 640 staff. This was a three stage hierarchical/corroborated evidence design where the 103 managers who had received the skills training not only reported on themselves, but also were reported upon by their own bosses and subordinates. This unusual research design was developed and carried out by a group of post-graduate students at the Bradford Management Centre.

The three overlapping and interlocking samples provided a total of 220 separate questionnaires. The findings showed that the managers who had been trained in staff development skill had displayed a significant, corroborated improvement in all the six rating scales of 'before and after' behaviour of the managers. These scales were based on the major elements of the skill of appraisal interviewing that were taught in the workshop, these were:

1 establishing suitable atmosphere and rapport
2 obtaining key information
3 determining and pursuing objectives
4 communication with the appraisee
5 motivating the appraisee
6 organizing and carrying out the interview.

The study also showed that managers in mid-career seemed to most from skill training of this kind. The general conclu- from this study was that the training not only raised f skill of the managers in staff development behaviour, but it also raised the expectations of staff for being managed more skilfully. This finding had important implications for changes in the content of the workshop and for the way the overall staff development scheme was presented to the members of the organization.

II
Impact of the training

Impact on managers

Before examining the actual consequences of this training it is important to stress that it is not without difficulties and dangers.

If the course merely heightened awareness of the many pitfalls which can trap the unwary interviewer it would be worthwhile. In practice it has done much more than this. In general there appears to be a tendency for managers who have undergone this experience to become more purposeful and certainly more sensitive in their handling of appraisals. Even if managers find it difficult to accept their inadequacies during the interview critique sessions, the survey indicates that it seems reasonable to assume that they will think about their performance privately afterwards. In this self-analysis process they will reach conclusions about their behaviour and postulate actions which can correct and improve their approach.

There are difficulties which arise out of managers' increased sensitivity and awareness. Maybe some managers, in certain circumstances, will be too tolerant, to the detriment of the subordinate's subsequent performance and the relationship between them. But in all behaviour changing and skill improving activities such as this there is always the risk of over-correction. People who are told that their sentences are too long often shorten them so much that their writing style becomes stilted, cramped and jerky. The results here are immediately obvious and can be put right by further small adjustments. In interviewing they are not so obvious and certainly would not be expected to appear immediately. The risk must therefore be accepted and tutors must apply whatever preventative treatment they can during the training interviews and analysis sessions. It is easy to spot over-reaction during these sessions and use observed incidences to point out its existence and discuss its changes with all participants. Again it seems reasonable to assume that the intelligent managers will guard against over-reaction and reduce it to a minimum, once they are aware of its insidious dangers.

To this extent improving appraisal by training interviewers must remain something of an act of faith. Tutors can observe technique improvements and apparent changes in attitudes and understanding. From this they can predict likely changes in behaviour and resultant improvement in the performance of those who are subsequently appraised by those who have undergone the training. The course of real interviews would be unduly influenced if tutors were present; maintenance of the new standard and continued improvement of skill must therefore be a self-checking process. The manager must constantly be able, with little effort, to monitor his performance against the standards set. In doing this he must make use of self-knowledge gained in the training, and take into account what he has learned about perception, the dangers of projecting his values on others and the need constantly to bear in mind that, in the appraisal situation, it is important to have as full a picture of the other's point of view even if you accept little or none of it. Common sense dictates that the course must provide as much self-checking information for managers as possible. This is the basis of the discussions on principles of interviewing; it threads right through all the analytical sessions. Constant reminders are given throughout the course about the need to be on the watch for signs which can enable the managers to check for themselves.

Finally, the need to remove illusions before any attempt is made to train managers in appraisal interviewing cannot be too strongly stressed. Unless and until this can be brought about little progress can be expected. Until the successful manager can be convinced that his understanding of himself and others is imperfect, he cannot be motivated to change his behaviour and cannot be convinced that he could be even more successful. Such a process will always be, at best, uncomfortable and at worst painful; it need never be brutal.

Turning to the impact in practice. First and foremost the very existence of the training imposed a responsibility on the part of the manager to approach interviews in a more purposeful way. Having the experience of being a subject, however artificial the circumstances may have been, gave the awareness of what was expected and the consequences of not doing it well. This need was heightened when the training had spread throughout the organization and most people knew the 'name of the game'. There being no escape the best thing to do was do it properly. Certainly this was an immediate effect, later confirmed by requests for 'refresher' sessions to help managers plan their interviews and concentrate upon strategies.

However, there is a much more fundamental aspect, that of important additional spin-off benefits. Because of the close involvement with the characters of the subjects and their circumstances in interviews, however fictitious, most managers were being forced to consider human behaviour and motivation in greater depth than ever before. The effects of different management styles were being demonstrated to them, and what could be achieved by encouraging participation. They were finding the value of altering their style to suit particular circumstances. As one manager said, 'As a result of the course it seems likely that I shall use more varied interviewing styles. I see that my present style is wholly benevolent/authoritarian and that the introduction of other styles could improve the effectiveness of my interviews.' This in turn led to the examination and discussion of management style within their own organizations.

This form of training is making managers much more aware of the importance of training in organic skills. It has done more perhaps than anything else in the training programme to arouse their interest in the study of motivation. This is why it links so closely with leadership, causing the subtitle to be added to this edition.

Impact on employees

Raising the expectations of staff for being managed more skilfully is mentioned in the previous chapter, but a word of warning is necessary. Many employees link increased interactive skill on the part of the manager with increased opportunities for them. In practice the opposite may be the case. It may be that the manager is now able to handle the weaker points of performance more elegantly, or to help the subordinate face the fact that there is little prospect of promotion. Perhaps it will be the first time that such aspects have been raised, whereas previously managers have, by sheer inability, conveyed a totally false impression of subordinates' performance or prospects.

Inconsistency amongst appraisers has created problems. Inevitably skills will differ widely; inevitably too, employees discuss their appraisals with each other, a point that is often forgotten by managers. There is therefore a danger that certain sections of the staff will lack the degree of openness and communication enjoyed by others and they will be disgruntled. A particular case in point occurred in an office whose staff were represented by a joint consultative committee. It became clear that one particular department was constantly dissatisfied with the way it was treated and by the lack of information which it had been given. This quickly became a schism in what was previously a happy and efficient office. Investigation showed that the manager of this department had slipped through the net when managers were being trained and, as is often the case, was the person who most needed it. If managers are permitted to escape, the organization allows this at its peril.

Most appraisers are themselves appraised; what is the effect therefore of both having had similar training? Will not the 'game' be recognized and the playing of it detract from the outcome? What happens when the appraisee has had the training and the appraiser has not? These are natural questions which have been met in practice. It has been found that far from being detrimental the reverse is the case. The fact that the 'game' is known promotes support for it from both parties and often the appraisee will help the appraiser in the interest of achieving a worthwhile outcome. One of the authors recalls that the personnel director who appraised him would preface the interview by saying 'I hate doing this because I haven't been on one of your courses'! Whether conscious or not, this gambit was brilliant. The only possible reaction to it was to do everything possible to help him!

Impact on procedures and systems

On the question of procedures and systems we soon ran into problems. The reward system demanded that an assessment should be made of the individual's performance to support the reward recommendation. This assessment was done on a form which sought information about the subordinate and a rating of his performance. It was subsequently passed up the line for approval and scrutiny, then returned to the manager who, at the time of the salary review, carried out an appraisal interview.

Our personnel management staff had for some time been unhappy with the procedure as the sequence Assessment—Appraisal meant that the manager was first making judgements, then seeking evidence and information to support them. They were also unhappy about the lack of information and evidence on the assessment form. All that had been achieved from this form in the past were scant and perhaps guarded comments which expanded *opinion* as to why a particular rating applied. They had not been able to make as good progress as they hoped in improving quality of information because of managers' lack of skill in appraisal interviewing.

An almost immediate reaction in the early days of the training course came strongly from managers who, realizing the fallacy of the old sequence, felt trapped at the idea of returning to it knowing it was now beneath their capacities. They also complained that the space provided on the old form was far too small for them to do justice to their assessments.

With managers pressing for change the climate was right for the personnel department to start introducing the changes it had already seen as desirable. The first step was to improve the assessment form. In the course we convey the strident message 'If you make judgements about people you must have evidence'. Managers are trained to tease out evidence on which to *base* rather than to *justify* judgements. It was now possible to make a natural transition from training to the work situation by providing an evidence-based form using much of the language of the training course. Later this form was made still more supportive to the managers' skill by asking such questions as 'What plans have you agreed to improve performance?' 'What are the views about career progress?'

The next step was to separate out the performance review from the salary review and move to the sequence Appraisal—Assessment. This took longer. It was necessary to make sure that the skill of the great majority of managers operating the system had been raised to cope with it. It was also necessary to see that through practice, a sufficiently open atmosphere between appraiser and appraised had been created for the new procedure to be immediately acceptable, if not overdue.

As the reader will have observed, the procedure evolved through pressure from managers themselves. It is unlikely that any other approach would have succeeded at that time. Latterly of course thinking has sharpened. The separating of assessment from development has been reinforced and the extent of the task expected of management has been understood. Whatever the eventual system, there is no short-cut to the ideal, but whatever that ideal is, it must be matched to the skills of the managers who have to operate it.

Impact on the organization

This information-based approach to staff development has repercussions throughout the organization. Once an organization is accustomed to making decisions about people based on real information collected from and about those people, it can then use the data generated for all human resources management decisions. Being more confident that the decisions will be sound also encourages taking more 'high-risk' decisions and moving away from the bland 'same-for-everyone' approach. For example:

REWARD DISTRIBUTION

After a sequence of active staff development reviews a manager will know thoroughly/accurately who is doing their job really well and who not so well. As there is an increasing tendency to apply additional financial rewards to high performers, being *certain* who they are, and the *degree* to which they contribute to the organization's success is an essential requirement for recognizing this special ability and effort. This recognition is not necessarily financial but will include all the other ways that managers have at their disposal to meet their staff's immediate needs. In other words, once individual differential ability and effort has been discriminated, differential effort can be applied to rewarding it. This is an important aspect of fairness in the social contract between employees and their work organization.

High performers

With the need to become more flexible and adaptive to the changing economic and technological conditions, identifying strengths and inclinations (both sometimes hidden) based on 'hard' information of the people able and willing to go with these changes is paramount. Staff appraisal delivers this information to the allocation or potential spotting procedure. Such data may just be the signal to enter an organization's assessment centre. It may be enough on which to take the risk to try out the person in another job or on a special project. The thorough sharing of current performance information must be the starting point for career development of the high-fliers!

Backbone staff

Every organization has a core of backbone staff who regularly and consistently achieve what is required of them, but who have little chance of, or even real wish for, promotion.

This poses problems of maintaining motivation for these essential and productive people. Precise information will enable managers to lead effectively through matching these people's true and realistic aspirations with equal understanding and commitment by the organization. Again, this is not necessarily through financial reward. Showing concern for and giving effort to the needs of diligent, perhaps long-serving, members of staff is crucial to maintaining the satisfaction and satisfactoriness of these staff. The more precisely this can be done, the more effective it will be.

Marginal performers

Understanding the real reasons for marginal, or even predicted marginal, performers and devising active plans to cope with them is an inevitable part of management's task. A sequence of behaviourally based development interviews can lift a level of performance from being inadequate to being acceptable. Just giving someone a rating of inadequacy and telling them 'to do something about it' is neither helpful nor precise enough to be effective. What is required is painstaking and patient accumulation and sharing of information. Where all this failed there is no option other than for the employee to leave. Doing this graciously and with a minimum loss of dignity has to be based on information which is clear and openly discussed between the leaver and the organization.

It is not only humanitarian issues that are involved. In such cases legislation requires compliance with a procedure for both verbal and written warnings to be issued and the provision of training to remedy deficiencies. Only when these deficiencies are carefully documented and discussed has the employer the evidence needed to demonstrate that dismissal was fair.

Review

This chapter has been devoted to the impact of a data-based approach on the skill of managing people.

Leadership must start at management of the individual since only by accurate knowledge of the individual's skills, aspirations and inclinations can the climate and conditions be set for people.

Unless and until this concept of data-based appraisal can be encouraged to grow within the manager, with the organization providing support and encouraging its use throughout, effective leadership is unlikely to exist.

Staff appraisal training is the way to bring about this first step.

Bibliography

The following books have been selected for further reading for students of the topic of staff appraisal and development. They range from the classic to the ordinary, from the mechanistic to the insightful and between them they represent a fair cover of recent alternative approaches to the topic.

ANSTEY E., FLETCHER C. and WALKER J. *Staff Appraisal and Development*, London, Allen and Unwin, 1976

CAMPBELL J. P., DUNNETTE M. D., LAWLER E. E. and WEICK K. E. *Managerial Behavior and Effectiveness*, New York, McGraw-Hill, 1970

CARROLL S. J. and SCHNEIER C. E. *Performance Appraisal and Review Systems*, Glenview, Illinois, Scott, Foresman, 1982

CONELLAN T. K. *How to Improve Human Performance: Behaviorism in Business and Industry*, New York, Harper and Row, 1978

CUMMINGS L. L. and SCHWAB D. P. *Performance in Organisations; Determinants and Appraisal*, Glenview, Illinois, Scott, Foresman, 1973

DEVRIES D. L., MORRISON A. M., SHULLMAN S. L. and GERLACH M. L. *Performance Appraisal on the Line*, New York, Wiley, 1981

GILL D. *Appraising Performance: Present Trends and the Next Decade*, London, Institute of Personnel Management, 1977

HONEY P. *Solving People Problems*, Maidenhead, McGraw-Hill, 1980

HUNT J. G., SEKARAN U. and SCHRIESHEIM C. A. *Leadership, Beyond Establishment Views*, Carbondale, Southern Illinois University Press, 1982

LATHAM G. P. and WEXLEY K. N. *Increasing Productivity Through Performance Appraisal*, Reading, Mass., Addison-Wesley 1981

MAGER R. F. and PIPE P. *Analysing Performance Problems*, Belmont, Calif., Pitman, 1970

PEDLAR M., BURGOYNE J. and BOYDELL T. *A Manager's Guide to Self-development*, Maidenhead, McGraw-Hill, 1978

SINGER E. J. *Effective Management Coaching*, 2nd ed., London, Institute of Personnel Management, 1979

STEWART V. and STEWART A. *Practical Performance Appraisal*, London, Gower, 1977

Tilley K. W. *Ed. Leadership and Management Appraisal*, London, English Universities Press, 1974

Wexley K. N. *and* Latham G. P. *Developing and Training Human Resources in Organisations*, Glenview, Illinois, Scott, Foresman, 1981

The following publications are by the staff and post-graduate students of the University of Bradford Management Centre, or are about the 'Bradford' approach to staff development. For ease of reading, no direct references to these publications have been made in the text. The concepts and data on which the material of this book is based have both stimulated and been stimulated by all of this work.

Alban-Metcalf B. M. *Leadership Theories and Their Implications for Managerial Skills*, Unpublished MBA dissertation, University of Bradford library, 1979

Alban-Metcalf B. M. 'Leadership Development: Towards an interpersonal skills training programme', *Journal of European Industrial Training*, 20 pp19–22, 1980

Alban-Metcalf B. M. *Micro-skills of Leadership*, Unpublished PhD Thesis, University of Bradford library, 1982

Alban-Metcalf B. M. 'Leadership: Extrapolation from theory and research to practical skills training', *Journal of Management Studies*, 19 pp295–305, 1982

Alban-Metcalf B. M. 'How relevant is leadership research to the study of managerial effectiveness: A critique and a suggestion', *Personnel Review*, 12 3, pp3–8, 1984

Alban-Metcalf B. M. 'Micro-skills of Leadership: A detailed analysis of the behaviour of managers in the appraisal interview' in Hunt J. G., Hosking D., Schriesheim C. A. *and* Stewart R. *Eds, Leaders and Managers: International Perspectives on Managerial Behavior and Leadership*, New York, Pergamon, 1984

Allinson C. W. 'Training in Performance Appraisal Interviewing; an evaluation study', *Journal of Management Studies*, 14, pp179–191 1977

Allinson C. W., Jackson A. P., Parkinson R. *and* Rix A. G. *A Study of the Effects of Training on Appraisal Interviewing in the Agrochemical Division of Fisons Limited*, University of Bradford, Human Resources Research Group, 1975

Bailey C. T. (*nee* Morrison). *The Measurement of Job Performance*, London, Gower, 1983

Bailey C. T. *and* Butcher D. J. 'Interpersonal skills training I: the nature of skill acquisition and its implications for training design and management', *Management Education and Development*, 14, pp48–54, 1983a

Bailey C. T. *and* Butcher D. J. 'Interpersonal skills training II: the trainers role', *Management Education and Development* 14, pp106–112, 1983b

BRADLEY, P. G. *Management by Objectives, an Appraisal,* Unpublished MSc dissertation, University of Bradford library, 1971

BRIDGE R. *The Determinants of a Staff Appraisal System* (in GPO), Unpublished MBA dissertation, University of Bradford library, 1979

CHAMBERS P. 'Maintenance: Machine and Man Both Need It', *British Plastics and Rubber* January 1978, pp38–40 1978

DONEGAN M. J. F. *and* ERSKINE M. *Report on Evaluation of Management Development Programme; Performance Appraisal Training in Evode Group of Companies,* Report for Rubber and Plastics Industry Training Board, 1977

ELLIS M. E. D. *Management Potential as a Concept in Personnel Management,* Unpublished MSc dissertation, University of Bradford library, 1975

GILL R. W. T. 'The in-tray (in-basket) exercise as a measure of management potential', *Journal of Occupational Psychology* 52, pp185–197, 1979

GILL R. W. T. *The Trainability Concept for Management Potential,* Unpublished PhD thesis, University of Bradford library, 1980

GILL R. W. T. 'A trainability concept for management potential and an empirical study of its relationship with intelligence for two managerial skills', *Journal of Occupational Psychology* 55, pp139–147, 1982

GILL R. W. T. *and* TAYLOR D. S. 'Training managers to handle discipline and grievance interviews', *Journal of European Training* 5, pp217–227, 1976

MORRISON C. T. *The Dimensionality and Subjectivity of Job Performance Measurement,* Unpublished PhD thesis, University of Bradford library, 1981

MORRISON C. T. *and* RANDELL G. A. *Problems in Developing Behaviourally Anchored Rating Scales,* University of Bradford Human Resources Group, 1977

NORRIS P. W. *A Study of the Development of a Staff Appraisal System in a Large Organization* (NHS), Unpublished MSc thesis, University of Bradford library, 1977

PARKINSON R. *Using performance reviews to develop managerial skills and organisations: An investigation of a training technique,* Paper presented to BPS Occupational Psychology Section Conference, Keele, Human Resources Research Group, University of Bradford, 1976

RANDELL G. A. 'The motor skills of man-management', *Management Decision* 9, pp31–39, 1971

RANDELL G. A. 'Performance appraisal, purposes, practices and conflicts', *Occupational Psychology* 47, pp221–224, 1973

RANDELL G. A. 'Staff appraisal and development through interviewing', *The Training Officer* 11, pp166–169, 1975

RANDELL G. A. 'Management selection and recruitment' in *Management Development and Training Handbook, Ed* TAYLOR B. *and* LIPPITT G. New York, McGraw-Hill, 1975, 2nd ed. 1983

RANDELL G. A. 'Interviewing at work' in *Psychology at Work, Ed* WARR P. B., Harmondsworth, Penguin, Rev. edtn 1978

RANDELL G. A. 'The skills of staff development' in *The Analysis of Social Skill, Ed.* SINGLETON W. T. *et al.,* New York, Plenum, 1979

RANDELL G. A. *Teaching high level skills to high level people,* Paper to Conference on Advances in Management Education, UMIST, University of Bradford Human Resources Research Group, 1981

RANDELL G. A. 'Management education and training' in *Management Skills: Vol. 3 in the Study of Real Skills, Ed.* SINGLETON W. T., Lancaster, MTP, 1981

RANDELL G. A. *and* STILL M. D. *Management Training Behaviour and Performance—Report to CAPITB,* University of Bradford Human Resources Research Group, 1973

ROMANO S. *Current Directions in Leadership Theory,* Unpublished MBA dissertation, University of Bradford library, 1982

RUSSELL N. P. *An Evaluation Study of a Management Development Programme,* Unpublished MSc dissertation, University of Aston library, 1977

SMITH J. H. *Performance Appraisals: a Problem of Validation,* Unpublished MBA dissertation, University of Bradford library, 1979

STILL M. D. 'Determinants of management training policies', *Journal of Business Policy* 24, 1972

TAYLOR D. S. *Performance Reviews: A Handbook for Tutors,* London, Institute of Personnel Management, 1976

TAYLOR D. S. *and* WRIGHT P. L. 'Training auditors in interviewing skills', *Journal of European Industrial Training* 1, pp6–16, 1977

TAYLOR D. S. *and* WRIGHT P. L. 'Influencing work performance: the development of diagnostic skills', *The Journal of Management Development* 1, pp44–50, 1982

TAYLOR S. G. *The Identification of Management Potential and its Relevance for the National Health Service,* Unpublished MBA dissertation, University of Bradford library, 1983

WEE Y. C. *Identification of Management Potential—A Concept for Singapore Management,* Unpublished MBA dissertation, University of Bradford library, 1978

WHITELAW M. *A Selected Bibliography of Material Relating to the Evaluation of Management Training,* University of Bradford Human Resources Research Group, 1971

WHITELAW M. *The Evaluation of Management Training—A Review,* London, Institute of Personnel Management, 1972

WRIGHT P. L. *and* TAYLOR D. S. *The Evaluation of a 'Pilot' Course in Interviewing Skills for Local Authority Auditors*, Human Resources Research Group, University of Bradford Management Centre, 1978

WRIGHT P. L. *and* TAYLOR D. S. 'The interpersonal skills of leadership: their analysis and training' Part I *Leadership and Organizational Development Journal* 2, 2, pp6–12, 1981a

WRIGHT P. L. *and* TAYLOR D. S. 'The interpersonal skills of leadership: their analysis and training' Part II *Leadership and Organizational Development Journal* 2, 3, pp2–6, 1981b

WRIGHT P. L. *and* TAYLOR D. S. *Improving Leadership Performance*, New York, Prentice Hall, 1984a

WRIGHT P. L. *and* TAYLOR D. S. 'The development of tutoring skills for interpersonal skills trainers', *Journal of European Industrial Training* (in press), 1984b

WRIGHT P. L. *and* TAYLOR D. S. 'Hiccups and nightmares: some problems in tutoring role play exercises', *Journal of European Industrial Training* (in press), 1984c

Appendix

Course Programme

DAY ONE

9.00–10.30	PURPOSE OF APPRAISALS —Skills of staff development
10.50–12.00	MANAGING APPRAISAL INTERVIEWS —Questioning and listening techniques
12.00–12.45	BRIEFING AND PREPARATION FOR FIRST PRACTICE INTERVIEW
12.45–13.45	LUNCH
13.45–14.45 14.45–15.45	PRACTICE INTERVIEWS 1 and 2
16.00–17.00	PRACTICE INTERVIEWS 3
17.00–18.15	ASSEMBLY ANALYSIS AND DISCUSSION
18.15–18.45	BRIEFING FOR SECOND DAY

DAY TWO

9.00–10.15	MOTIVATIONAL FACTORS IN STAFF DEVELOPMENT
10.15–11.00	BRIEFING AND PREPARATION FOR SECOND PRACTICE INTERVIEW
11.00–12.00 12.00–13.00	PRACTICE INTERVIEWS 4 and 5
13.00–14.00	LUNCH
14.00–15.00	PRACTICE INTERVIEWS 6
15.00–16.00	ASSEMBLY ANALYSIS AND DISCUSSION